J. W. Bischoff

Gospel Bells

A Collection of New and Popular Songs for the use of Sabbath schools and

Gospel Meetings

J. W. Bischoff

Gospel Bells

A Collection of New and Popular Songs for the use of Sabbath schools and Gospel Meetings

ISBN/EAN: 9783337181765

Printed in Europe, USA, Canada, Australia, Japan

Cover: Foto ©Lupo / pixelio.de

More available books at **www.hansebooks.com**

GOSPEL BELLS.

A COLLECTION OF

NEW AND POPULAR SONGS

FOR THE USE OF

SABBATH SCHOOLS AND GOSPEL MEETINGS.

BY

PROF. J. W. BISCHOFF, OTIS F. PRESBREY

AND

REV. J. E. RANKIN, D. D.

CHICAGO·
THE WESTERN SUNDAY SCHOOL PUBLISHING CO.,
1880

EDITOR'S PREFACE.

The editors of **GOSPEL BELLS** have, for several years, been associated in conducting the service of song in one of the larger congregations in this country. This association has educated them to a better knowledge of the wants of God's people, and especially of God's little people, in the matter of hymns and music. And they take great pleasure in presenting this volume to the public, as at once a memorial of this kindly association, and in some true sense the ripe fruit of it. With greeting to the many old friends made for them, by previous labors in this direction, and to new friends, whom they modestly hope will be made by this collection, and with thanks to the many authors and composers who have so generously aided them in this work, they sign their names to this preface.

J. W. BISCHOFF,
O. F. PRESBREY,
J. E. RANKIN.

N. B.—It will be understood that the original material of this collection is copyright property, which the authors and composers alone claim the right to control.

Entered according to Act of Congress, A. D. 1880, by J. W. BISCHOFF, OTIS F. PRESBREY and J. E. RANKIN, in the office of the Librarian of Congress, at Washington.

GOSPEL BELLS.

No. 1. Tell Me More, Still More of Jesus.

"Thy name is as ointment poured forth."—CANT. i. 3.

J. E. RANKIN, D, D. *Moderato.* KARL REDEN.

1. Tell me more, still more of Je - sus, Let me hear His pre-cious name!
2. Tell me more, still more of Je - sus, How it calms my troubled soul!
3. Tell me more, still more of Je - sus, 'Tis the sweet-est name I know;
4. Tell me more, still more of Je - sus, How He grows up-on my thought!
5. Tell me more, still more of Je - sus, Tell it, to my lat - est breath;
6. Tell me more, still more of Je - sus, 'Tis the end-less theme a - bove;

Pour it forth, a-gain, as perfume, Sweeter, sweet-er, tho', the same.
I can nev - er, nev-er wea-ry, I can nev - er know the whole.
Whom have I in heav'n a - bove Him, Whom have I on earth be-low?
Tell me, tell me all the won-ders That His love for me has wrought.
Sweet it is in life to know Him, Sweeter, sweet - er still in death.
How He sought us, how He bought us, What the ran-som of His love.

Chorus. *Repeat pp.*

Tell me more, tell me more, Still more of Je - sus, Tell me more.

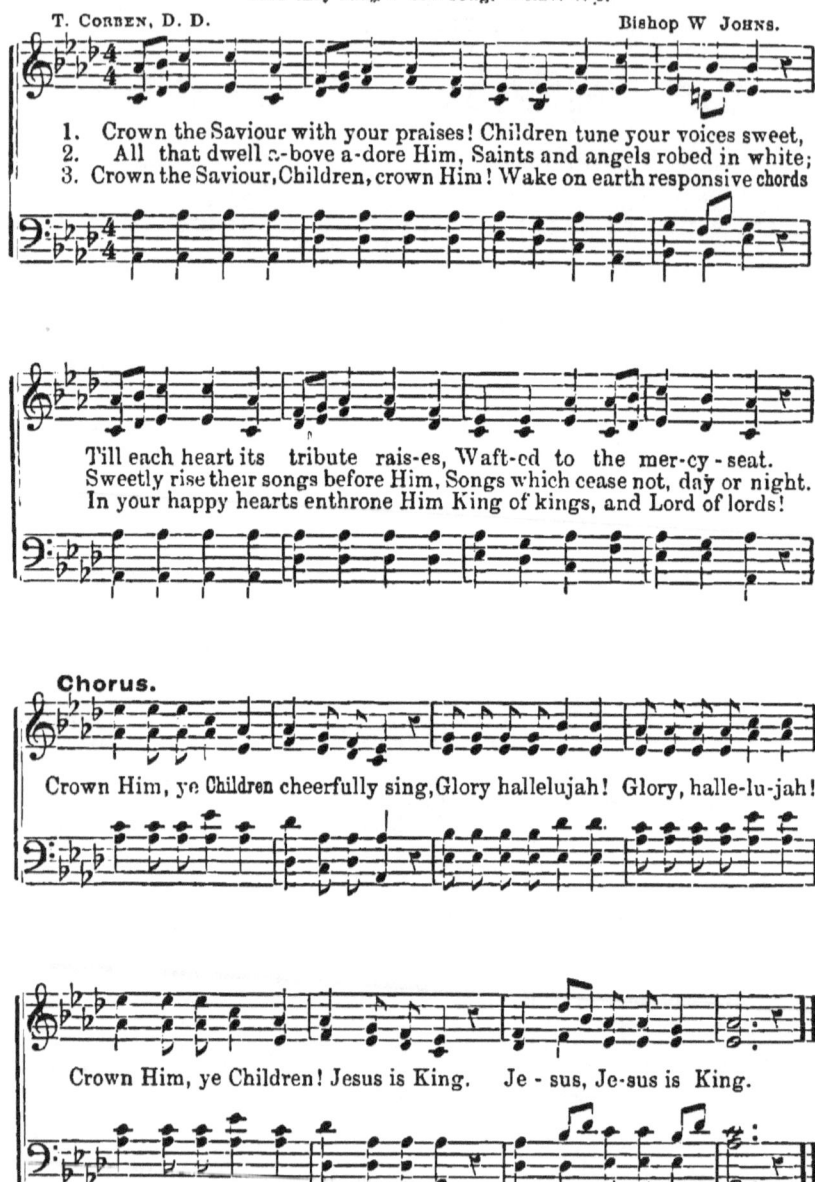

My Heavenly Home--Concluded.

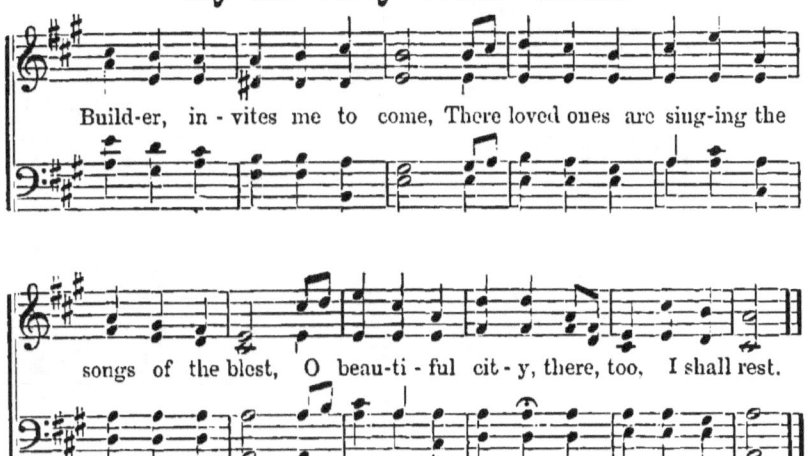

Build-er, in-vites me to come, There loved ones are sing-ing the songs of the blest, O beau-ti-ful cit-y, there, too, I shall rest.

No. 5. The Lord Will Provide.

"For He careth for you."—1 PET. v. 7.

Mrs. M. A. W. COOK.   E. S. LORENZ, by per.

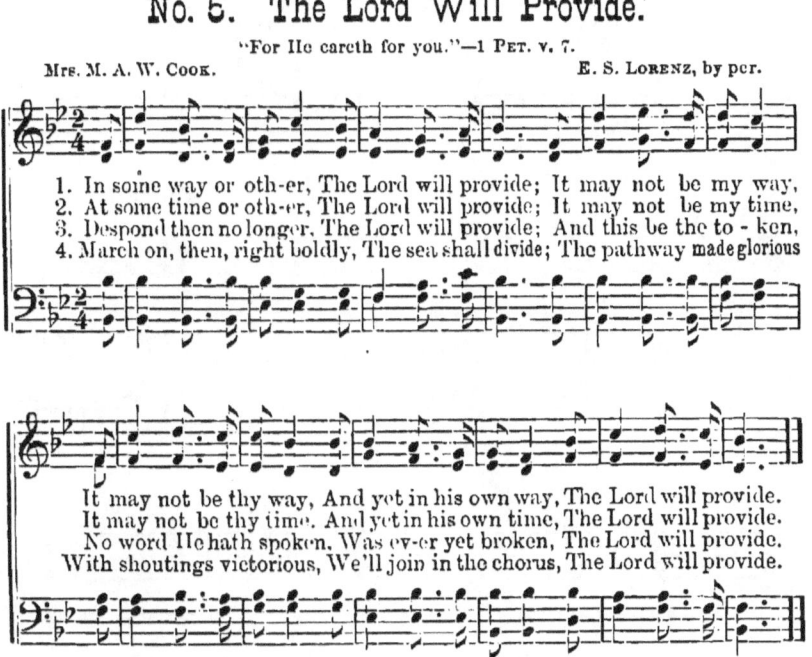

1. In some way or oth-er, The Lord will provide; It may not be my way,
2. At some time or oth-er, The Lord will provide; It may not be my time,
3. Despond then no longer, The Lord will provide; And this be the to-ken,
4. March on, then, right boldly, The sea shall divide; The pathway made glorious

It may not be thy way, And yet in his own way, The Lord will provide.
It may not be thy time, And yet in his own time, The Lord will provide.
No word He hath spoken, Was ev-er yet broken, The Lord will provide.
With shoutings victorious, We'll join in the chorus, The Lord will provide.

No. 7. Thou Know'st All Things, Is It I?

"And every one of them began to say unto Him, Lord, is it I?"—MATT. xxvi. 22.

J. E. RANKIN, D. D.   J. W. BISCHOFF.

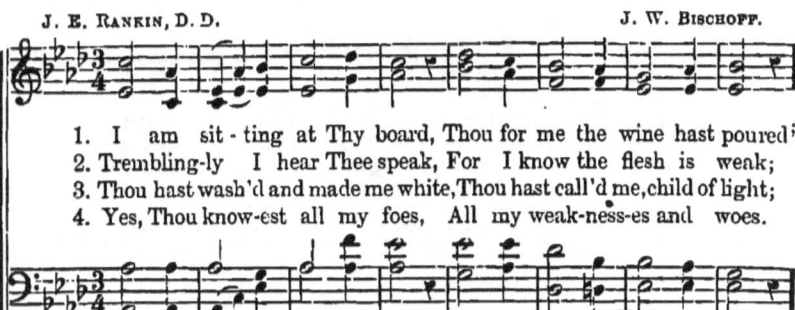

1. I am sit-ting at Thy board, Thou for me the wine hast poured;
2. Trembling-ly I hear Thee speak, For I know the flesh is weak;
3. Thou hast wash'd and made me white, Thou hast call'd me, child of light;
4. Yes, Thou know-est all my foes, All my weak-ness-es and woes.

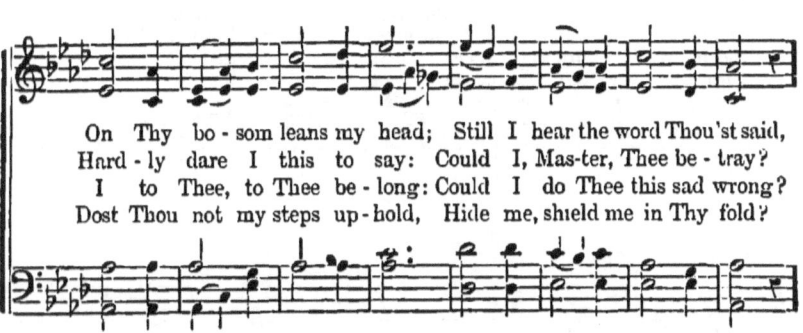

On Thy bo-som leans my head; Still I hear the word Thou'st said,
Hard-ly dare I this to say: Could I, Mas-ter, Thee be-tray?
I to Thee, to Thee be-long: Could I do Thee this sad wrong?
Dost Thou not my steps up-hold, Hide me, shield me in Thy fold?

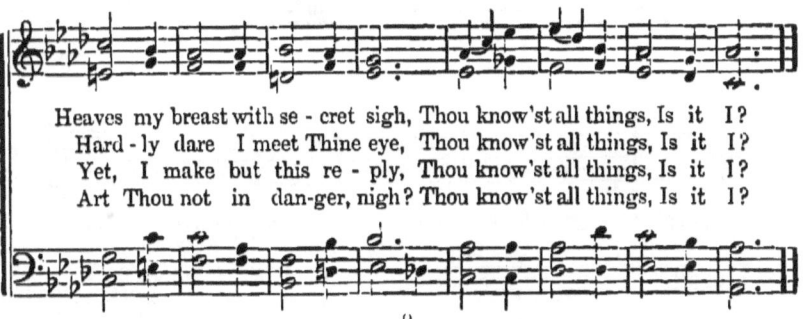

Heaves my breast with se-cret sigh, Thou know'st all things, Is it I?
Hard-ly dare I meet Thine eye, Thou know'st all things, Is it I?
Yet, I make but this re-ply, Thou know'st all things, Is it I?
Art Thou not in dan-ger, nigh? Thou know'st all things, Is it I?

No. 8. Unto The Lamb.

"And they sung the song of Moses and the song of the Lamb."—Rev. xv. 3.

S. WESLEY MARTIN.

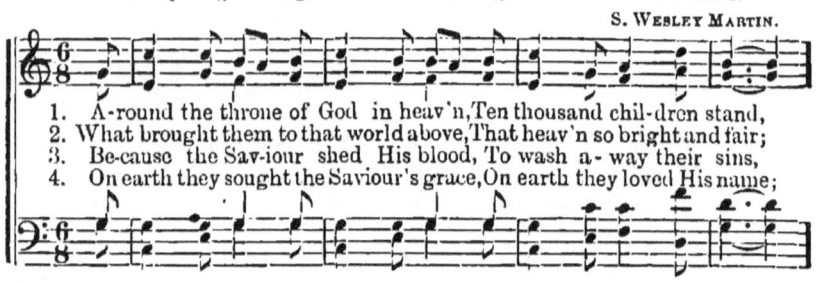

1. A-round the throne of God in heav'n, Ten thousand chil-dren stand,
2. What brought them to that world above, That heav'n so bright and fair;
3. Be-cause the Sav-iour shed His blood, To wash a-way their sins,
4. On earth they sought the Saviour's grace, On earth they loved His name;

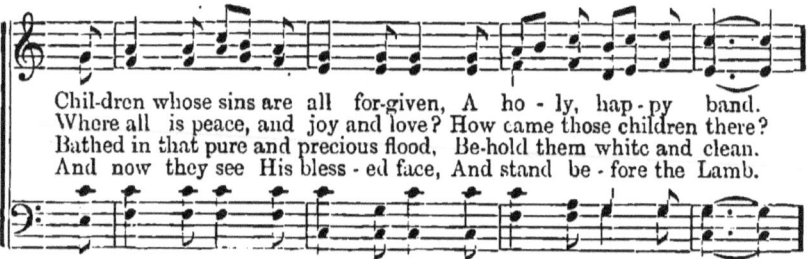

Chil-dren whose sins are all for-given, A ho-ly, hap-py band.
Where all is peace, and joy and love? How came those children there?
Bathed in that pure and precious flood, Be-hold them white and clean.
And now they see His bless-ed face, And stand be-fore the Lamb.

Chorus.

Sing-ing glo-ry, sing-ing glo-ry, Glo-ry, glo-ry, glo-ry,

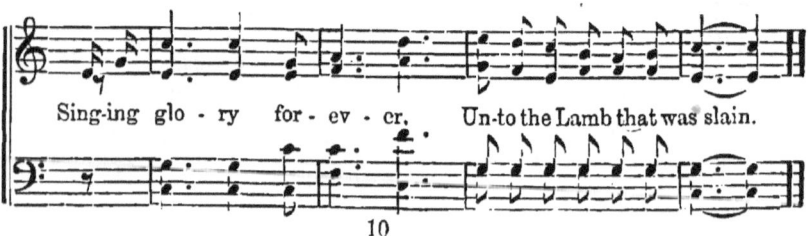

Sing-ing glo-ry for-ev-er, Un-to the Lamb that was slain.

No. 9. Can You Point a Lost Soul to the Saviour?

"Behold the Lamb of God."—JOHN i. 36.

Rev. J. E. RANKIN, D. D. Rev. S. MORRISON.

1. Can you point a lost soul to the Sav-iour? A soul that is sin-ful and
2. Oh, my heart it is heav-y with sor - row! My eyes are o'erflowing with
3. I once heard, I once heard of this Saviour, In childhood, a long time a-
4. Can you point a lost soul to the Sav-iour? My heart, it can struggle no

blind? Can you tell me where to find Him? He is said to be meek and
tears: But, a - las! not floods of weep-ing Can a - tone for my mis-spent
go: How our stripes were laid up-on Him: But, it went like the melt-ing
more: I am weak, and blind and sin-ful, Can you lead me un - to the

kind. But, oh, He is pure and ho - ly, And I am all vile with sin; But
years. For one of my sins, no an-swer Have I, that I dare to speak; But,
snow, The thought of my sins I stifled; The tho't of His love, the same; But,
door? The word I shall speak is mercy! And that, do you think He'll know? Thy

if I draw near, do you think He will hear, And rise and will let me in?
if I draw near, do you think He will hear, I'll find, if of Him I seek?
if I draw near, do you think He will hear, And blot out my sin and shame?
sins, will He say, I have washed them away, I've washed them as white as snow!

No. 11. It is I, O Soul Dismayed.

"It is I, be not afraid."—MATT xiv. 27.

J. E. RANKIN, D. D.   W. A. OGDEN.

1. Thou art walk-ing, O my Sav-iour, Walking on my troubled sea;
2. Thou art walk-ing, O my Sav-iour, Through the vale of tears with me;
3. With me wilt thou walk, my Saviour, Through the shades of coming death?
4. With thee shall I walk, my Saviour, Walk for aye with thee in white;

Thro' the lift-ing mists of sor-row, Lo, thy king-ly form I see.
Nor hast thou, thy-self for-got-ten Shades of dark Geth-sem-a-ne.
And up-on thy faith-ful bo-som, Shall I breathe my last, last breath?
Meet shall I be to in-her-it With the bloodwashed saints in light?

Chorus.

"It is I," I hear thee say, "Strength I'll e-qual to thy day; It is I, O soul dismayed, Be not a-fraid."

"It is I," I hear thee say,
"It is I, O soul dismayed,"

I Cannot Sing as Angels Sing—Concluded.

Chorus.

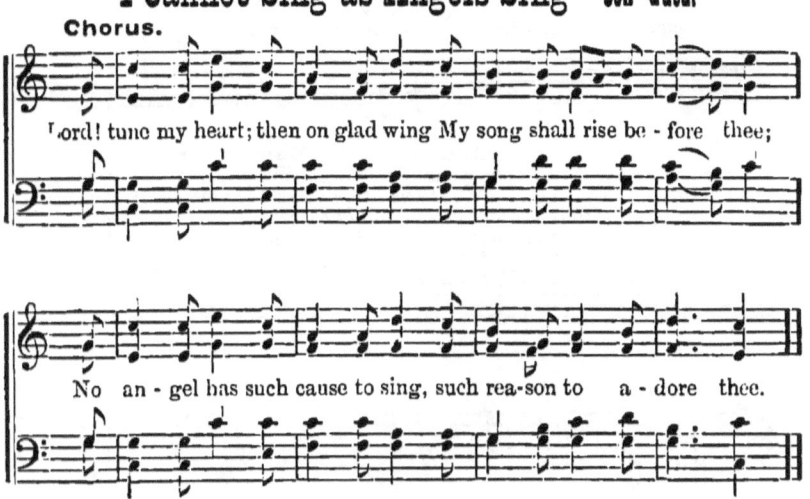

Lord! tune my heart; then on glad wing My song shall rise be-fore thee;
No an-gel has such cause to sing, such rea-son to a-dore thee.

No. 13. Art Thou Longing?

Rev. S. C. Morgan, "I will give you rest."—Matt. xi. 28. Ira D. Sankey.

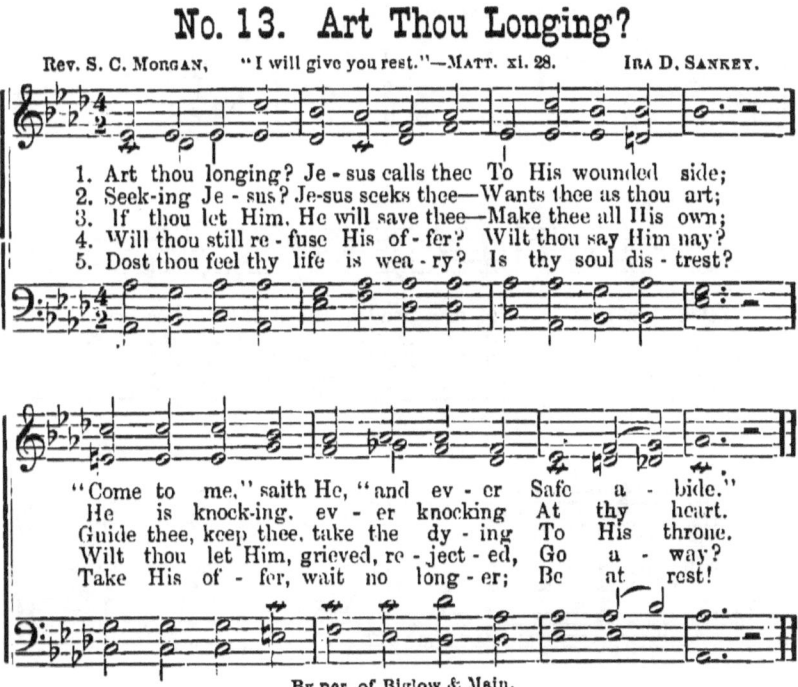

1. Art thou longing? Je-sus calls thee To His wounded side;
2. Seek-ing Je-sus? Je-sus seeks thee—Wants thee as thou art;
3. If thou let Him, He will save thee—Make thee all His own;
4. Will thou still re-fuse His of-fer? Wilt thou say Him nay?
5. Dost thou feel thy life is wea-ry? Is thy soul dis-trest?

"Come to me," saith He, "and ev-er Safe a-bide."
He is knock-ing, ev-er knocking At thy heart.
Guide thee, keep thee, take the dy-ing To His throne.
Wilt thou let Him, grieved, re-ject-ed, Go a-way?
Take His of-fer, wait no long-er; Be at rest!

By per. of Biglow & Main.

No. 14. Are You Ready, Children, Ready?

R. E. JEREMY. "All things are ready, come."—MATT. xxii. 4. M. SAMUELS.

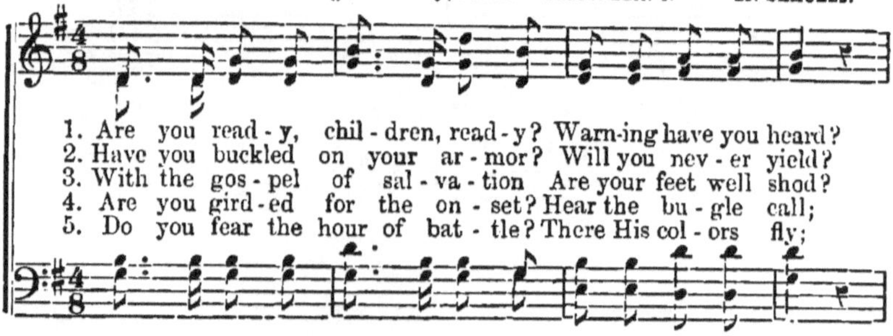

1. Are you read-y, chil-dren, read-y? Warn-ing have you heard?
2. Have you buckled on your ar-mor? Will you nev-er yield?
3. With the gos-pel of sal-va-tion Are your feet well shod?
4. Are you gird-ed for the on-set? Hear the bu-gle call;
5. Do you fear the hour of bat-tle? There His col-ors fly;

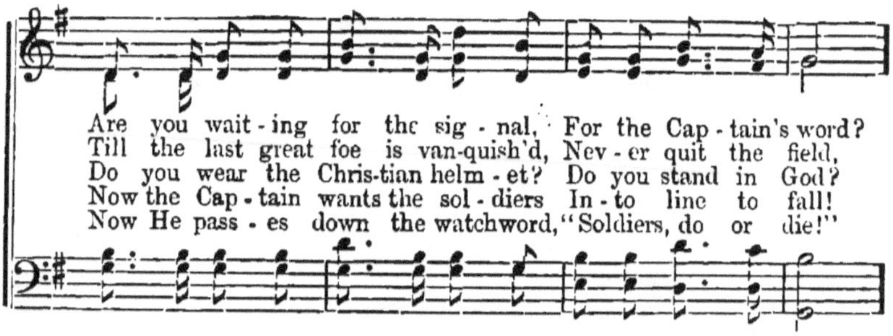

Are you wait-ing for the sig-nal, For the Cap-tain's word?
Till the last great foe is van-quish'd, Nev-er quit the field,
Do you wear the Chris-tian helm-et? Do you stand in God?
Now the Cap-tain wants the sol-diers In-to line to fall!
Now He pass-es down the watchword, "Soldiers, do or die!"

Chorus.

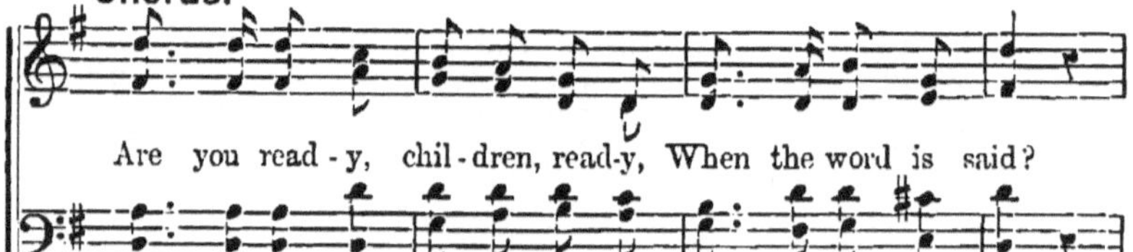

Are you read-y, chil-dren, read-y, When the word is said?

Will you move, then, firm and stead-y, With u-nit-ed tread?

No. 15. Beautiful the Little Hands.

"Whatsoever thy hand findeth to do, do it with thy might."—Eccles. ix. 10.

T. Corben, D. D. Bishop W. Johns.

1. Beau-ti-ful the lit-tle hands, That ful-fill the Lord's commands;
2. All the lit-tle hands were made, Je-sus' pre-cious cause to aid;
3. All the lit-tle lips should pray To the Sav-iour, ev-'ry day;
4. What your lit-tle hands can do, That the Lord in-tends for you;

Beau-ti-ful the lit-tle eyes, Kin-dled with light from the skies.
All the lit-tle hearts to beat Warm in His ser-vice so sweet.
All the lit-tle feet should go Swift on His er-rands be-low.
Make that thing your first de-light, Do it to Him with your might.

Chorus.

Beau-ti-ful, beau-ti-ful lit-tle hands, That ful-fill the Lord's commands;

Beau-ti-ful, beau-ti-ful lit-tle eyes, Kindled with light from the skies.

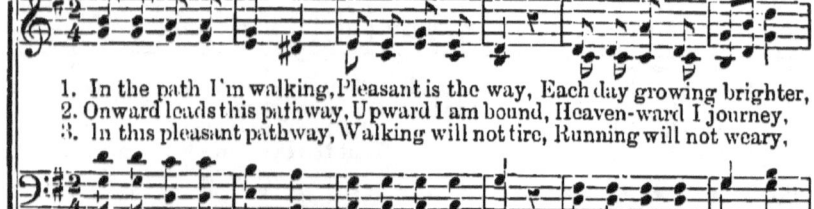
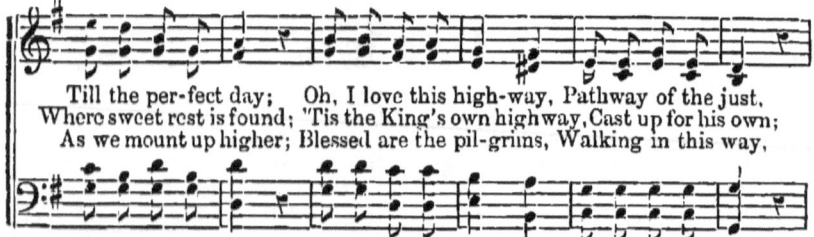

No. 17. I Am Praying for You.

Evening, and morning, and at noon, will I pray.—Psalms, 55:17.

S. O'Maley Cluff. Ira D. Sankey, by per.

1. I have a Saviour, He's pleading in glory: A dear, loving Saviour, tho' earth-friends be few; And now He is watching in tenderness o'er me, And oh, that my Saviour were your Saviour, too! For you I am praying, For you I am praying, For you I am praying, I'm praying for you.

2. I have a Father: to me He has given
A hope for eternity, blessed and true,
And soon will He call me to meet Him in Heaven—
But oh that He'd let me bring you with me, too!

3. I have a robe: 'tis resplendent in whiteness,
Awaiting in glory my wondering view;
Oh, when I receive it, all shining in brightness,
Dear friend, could I see you receiving one, too!

4. I have a peace: it is calm as a river—
A peace that the friends of this world never knew;
My Saviour alone is its Author and Giver;
And, oh, could I know it was given to you!

5. When Jesus has found you, tell others the story
That my loving Saviour is your Saviour, too;
Then pray that your Saviour may bring them to glory,
And prayer will be answered—'twas answered for you!

From Crystal Songs, by permission.

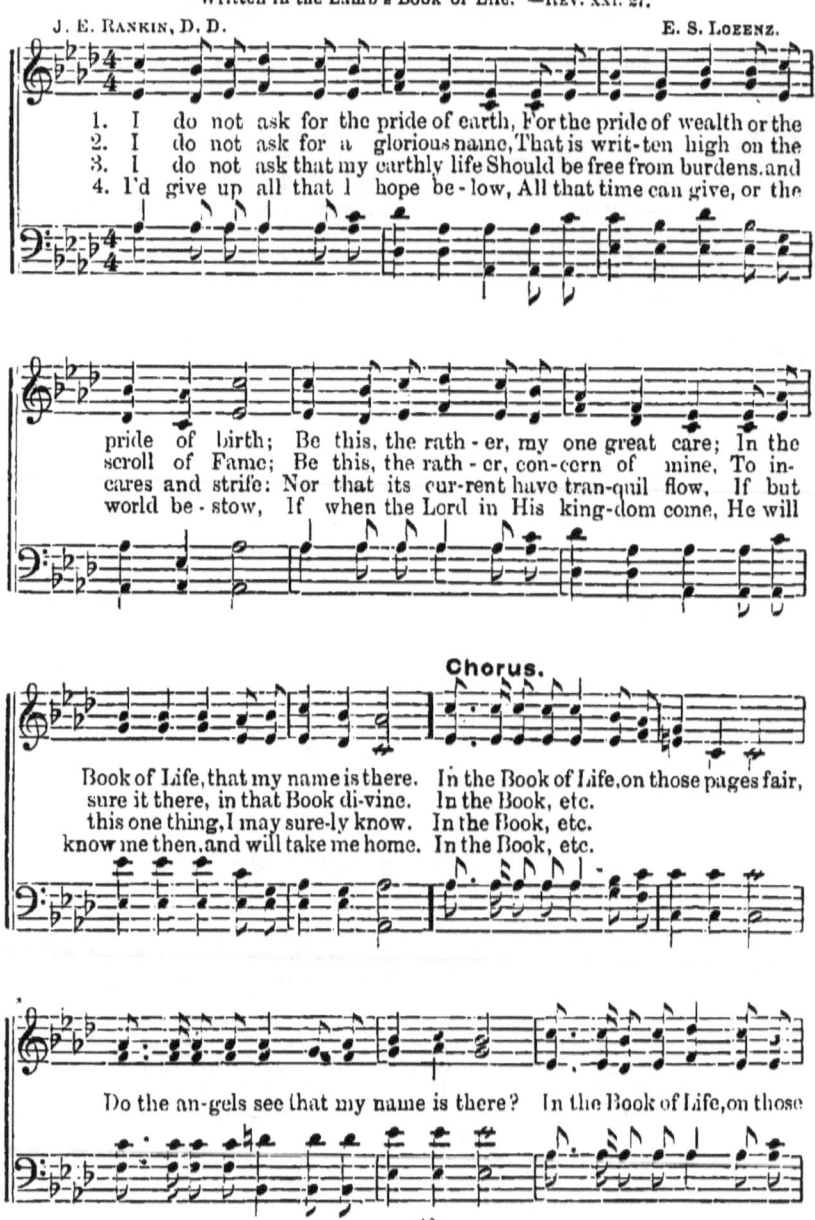

Is It There ? Written There ?—Concluded.

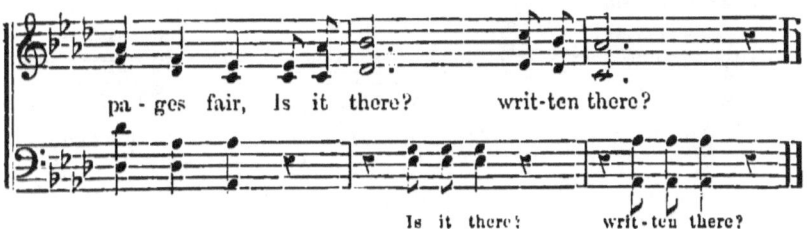

No. 19. The Wide, Wide World.

"The Lord alone did lead him."—DEUT. xxxii. 12.

Rev. W. O. CUSHING.   Rev. C. S. MEILY, by per.

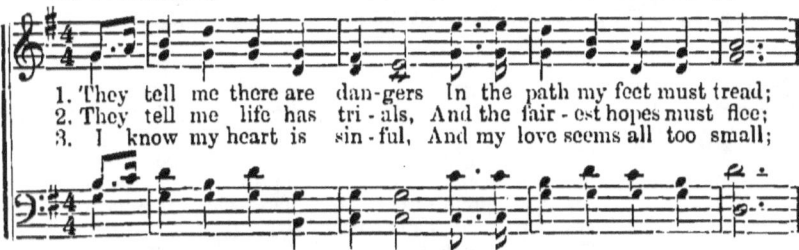

1. They tell me there are dangers In the path my feet must tread;
2. They tell me life has trials, And the fairest hopes must flee;
3. I know my heart is sinful, And my love seems all too small;

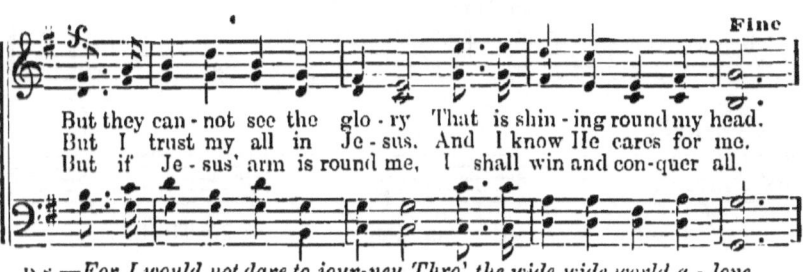

But they cannot see the glory That is shining round my head.
But I trust my all in Jesus, And I know He cares for me.
But if Jesus' arm is round me, I shall win and conquer all.

D.S.—For I would not dare to journey Thro' the wide, wide world alone.

Chorus.   D.S.

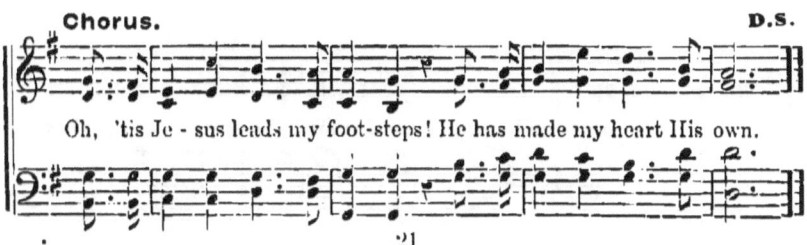

Oh, 'tis Jesus leads my footsteps! He has made my heart His own.

All Praise and All Majesty--Concluded.

peace in be-liev-ing, And sweetly each moment I'm trusting in Him.

No. 21. Jesus is Calling Thee.

"Ho! every one that thirsteth."—Isa. lv. 1.

T. T. Price.   Wm. W. Bentley, by per.

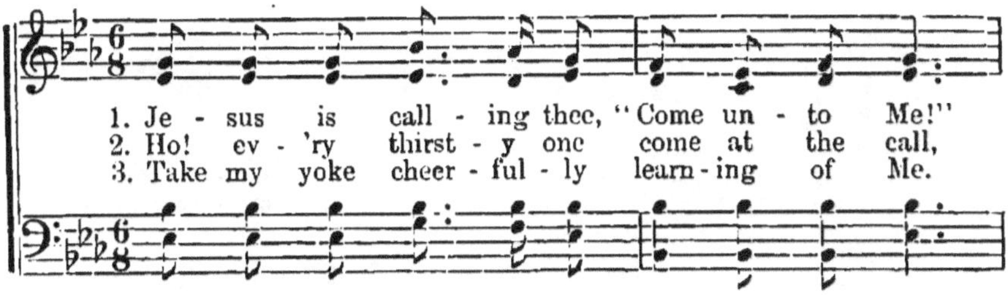

1. Je - sus is call - ing thee, "Come un - to Me!"
2. Ho! ev - 'ry thirst - y one come at the call,
3. Take my yoke cheer - ful - ly learn - ing of Me.

Mer - cy is offered thee, boundless and free. Come, all who labor here.
Streams of sal-va-tion flow free-ly for all. This is His call to thee,
Meek - ly and will-ing-ly trust and be free. Eas - y my yoke shall be:

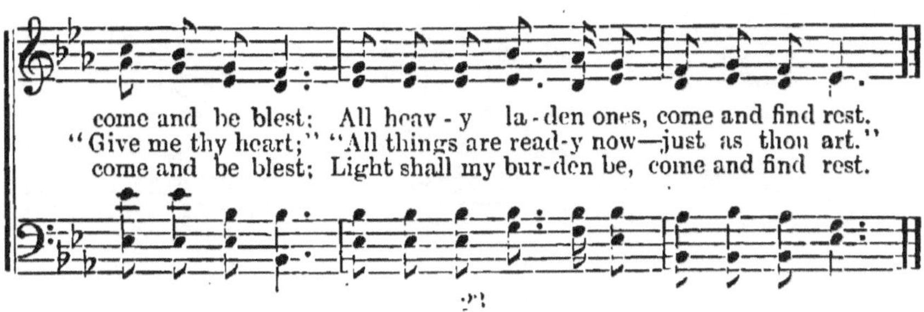

come and be blest; All heav - y la - den ones, come and find rest.
"Give me thy heart;" "All things are read-y now—just as thou art."
come and be blest; Light shall my bur-den be, come and find rest.

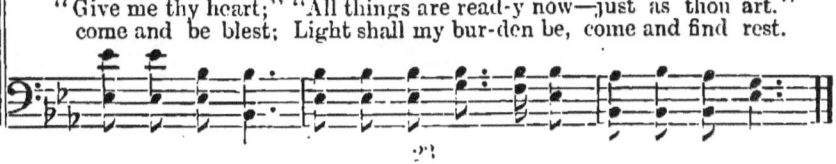

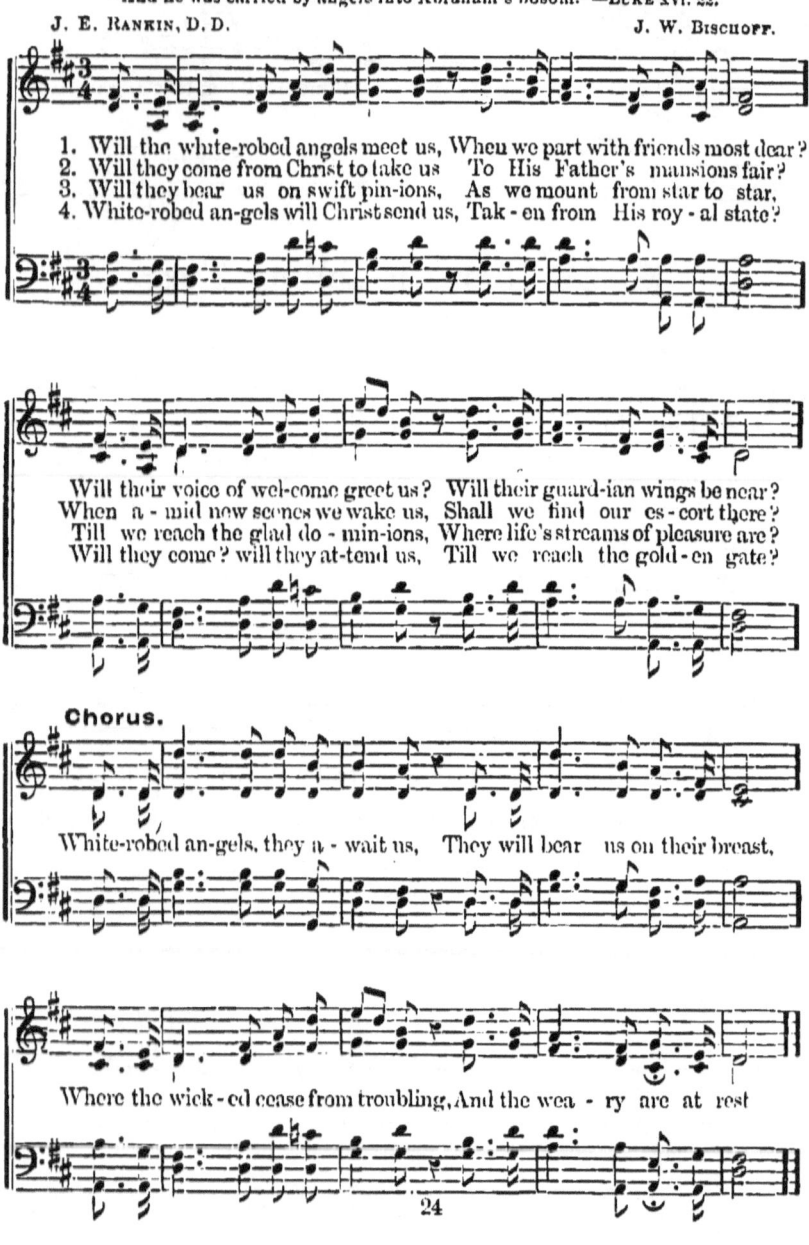

No. 24. I'll Sing for Jesus.

"To whom be praise and dominion forever and ever."—1 PET. iv. 11.

Rev. T. C. READE. J. H. ANDERSON, by per.

1. I'll sing for Je-sus while I've breath, I'll sing Him when I die;
2. When sink-ing un-der sin and grief, No oth-er help was nigh;
3. My troubled soul found sweet repose, While trusting in His blood,

His lov-ing kind-ness af-ter death I'll herald through the sky.
'Twas Je-sus came to my re-lief, 'Twas He who heard my cry.
And from the depths of sin a-rose, To dwell with Christ in God.

Chorus.

Sweet Sav - iour mine, I'll sing of thy wondrous love; I'll
Sweet Saviour, Saviour mine, I'll sing of thy wondrous love, wondrous love, I'll

serve Thee still, And I'll praise Thee up a-bove.
serve, yes, I'll serve thee still, serve thee still, And I'll praise thee up above, up a-bove.

No. 25. Go Wash in the Stream.

R. TORREY, Jr.   "A fountain is opened for sin."—ZECH. xiii, 1.   I. BALTZALL.

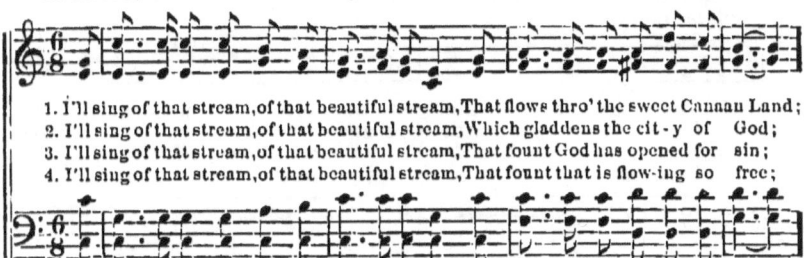

1. I'll sing of that stream, of that beautiful stream, That flows thro' the sweet Canaan Land;
2. I'll sing of that stream, of that beautiful stream, Which gladdens the cit-y of God;
3. I'll sing of that stream, of that beautiful stream, That fount God has opened for sin;
4. I'll sing of that stream, of that beautiful stream, That fount that is flow-ing so free;

Its waters gleam bright in their heav-en-ly light, And rip-ple o'er the gold-en sand.
It flows from the throne of the Fa-ther, a-lone; And spreads its sweet waters a-broad.
That stream from His side who for sinners once died: He's healed, who but plunges therein
I'll sing of that flood, which is crimsoned with blood, From sin, that has cleansed even me.

Chorus.

Go wash in that beautiful stream...... Go wash in that beau-ti-ful stream......
         Wash in the beau-ti-ful stream,   Wash in the beau-ti-ful stream,

Its wa-ters so free, are flow-ing for thee; Go, wash in that beauti-ful stream.

No. 27. Repeat the Sweet Story.

"Christ Jesus came into the world to save sinners, of whom I am chief."—1 Tim. i. 15

Rev. J. B. Atchinson.   Pearl J. Sprague.

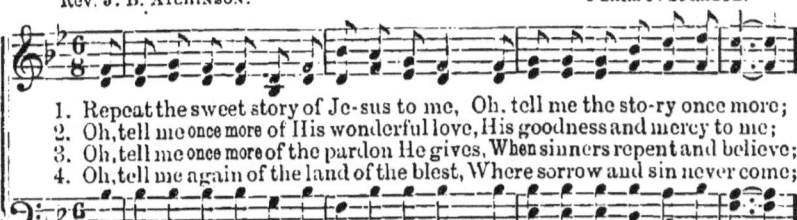

1. Repeat the sweet story of Je-sus to me, Oh, tell me the sto-ry once more;
2. Oh, tell me once more of His wonderful love, His goodness and mercy to me;
3. Oh, tell me once more of the pardon He gives, When sinners repent and believe;
4. Oh, tell me again of the land of the blest, Where sorrow and sin never come;

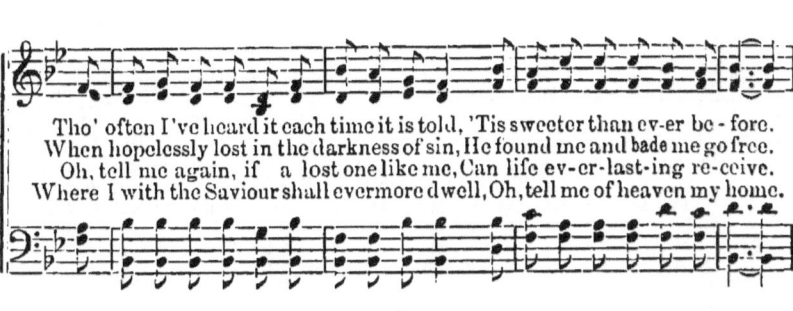

Tho' often I've heard it each time it is told, 'Tis sweeter than ev-er be-fore.
When hopelessly lost in the darkness of sin, He found me and bade me go free.
Oh, tell me again, if a lost one like me, Can life ev-er-last-ing re-ceive.
Where I with the Saviour shall evermore dwell, Oh, tell me of heaven my home.

Chorus.

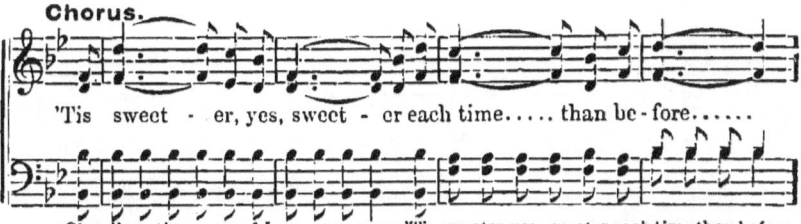

'Tis sweet - er, yes, sweet - er each time..... than be - fore......
Oh, tell me the sto-ry of Jesus once more, 'Tis sweeter, yes, sweeter each time than before.

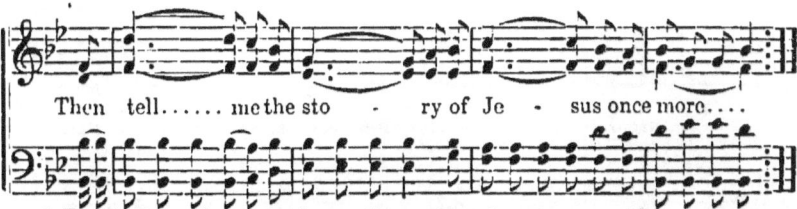

Then tell...... me the sto - ry of Je - sus once more....

1. How He died on the tree for sin-ners like me, Oh, tell me the sto-ry of Jesus once more.
2. How His wonderful love bro't Him from above, Oh, tell me, etc.
3. Of the Sav-iour of men, oh, tell it a-gain, Oh, tell me, etc.
4. Where I with the blest shall ev - er-more rest, Oh, tell me, etc.

No. 29. Faith.

"What time I am afraid, I will trust in Thee."—Ps. lvi. 3.

Mrs. C. S. SHACKLOCK. J. W. BISCHOFF.

1. The sky is o-ver-cast with clouds of gloom, The storm is nigh;
   On - ly thy presence can the night il-lume; To Thee I fly!
   Thy voice can bid the rag - ing temp - est cease,
   And fill my trou-bled heart with per - fect peace.

2. Tho' faint and weary with the con - flict long, I will not fear;
   I safe-ly pass the foaming waves among, When thou art near;
   Sav - iour di - vine! O help the sor - row - ing.
   To thy dear cross still trust - ing - ly I cling.

3. Thou art my an-chor; tho' the dis-tant land I can - not see,
   And darkness gathers round, thy guiding hand Still lead - eth me;
   I know the ha - ven of my rest is near;
   Safe in thy shel - tering care I can - not fear.

4. I thought not of the ref - uge of thy cross, When calm the sea;
   When tempest-toss'd, oppress'd with grief and loss, I fled to Thee;
   Sav - iour, to Thee I lift my stream-ing eyes,
   On Thee a - lone my soul for aid re - lies.

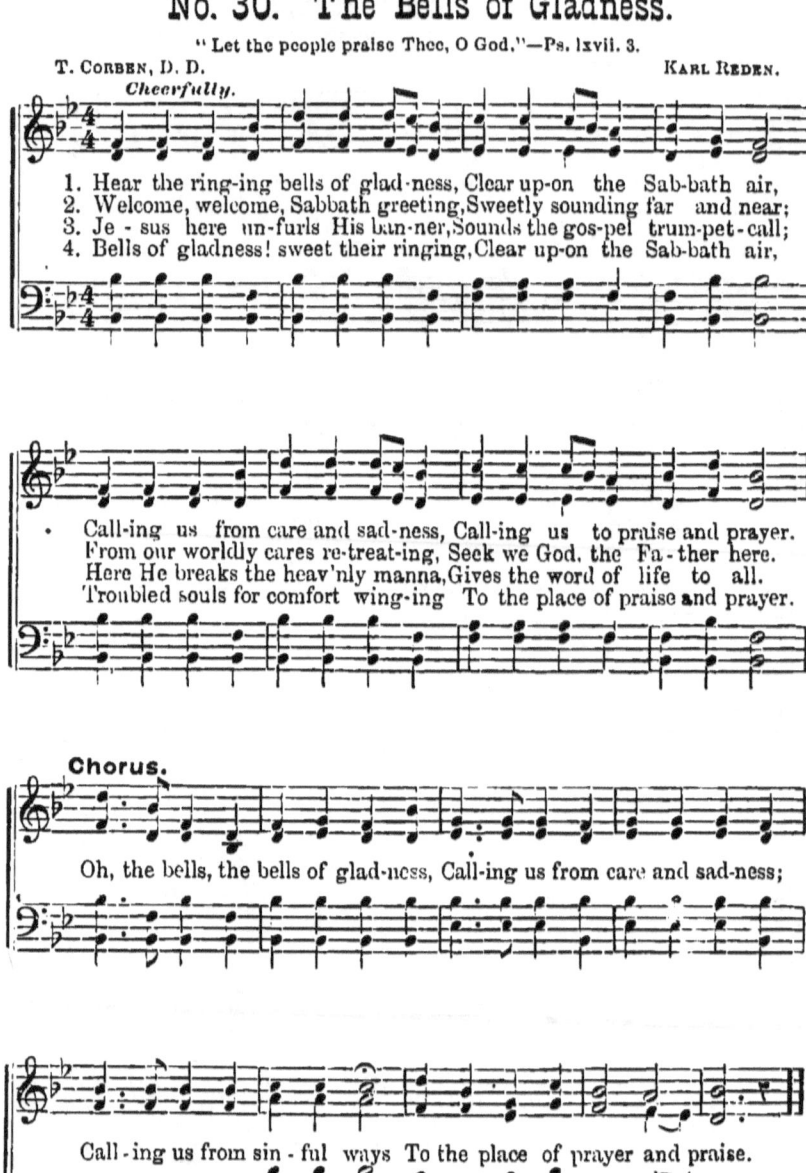

No. 32. White as Snow.

Though your sins be as scarlet, they shall be as white as snow.—Isa., 1:18.

J. H. Tenney.

1. "White as snow!" can my trans-gres-sions Thus be whol-ly wash'd a-way! Leav-ing not a trace be-hind them, Like a cloud-less sum-mer day.
2. "White as snow!" O, what a prom-ise For the heav-y lad-en breast! When by faith the soul re-ceives it, Wea-ri-ness is chang'd to rest.
3. Yes, at once, and that com-plete-ly, Thro' the blood of Christ, I know All my sins, tho' red like crim-son, May be-come as white as snow.

"White as snow!" "White as snow!" "White as snow!" "White as snow!" Je-sus cleans-es white as snow! Tho' your sins be red like crim-son, they shall be as white as snow.

From Crystal Songs, by permission.

No. 34. I Love the Dear Saviour.

"Lord, Thou knowest that I love Thee."—JOHN xxi. 15.

R. E. JEREMY.   M. SAMUELS.

1. I love the dear Sav-iour, In Beth-le-hem born;
2. I love the dear Sav-iour, Who healed all the blind,
3. I love the dear Sav-iour, For chil-dren He died;

His cra-dle, a man-ger, His lot, so for-lorn:
The sick and the crip-pled He ev-er could find:
With scour-ges, they scourged Him. And then cru-ci-fied;

Tho' heav-en's bright an-gels Came, sing-ing in air,
Who took lit-tle chil-dren, Looked up-ward and prayed;
His blood is the fount-ain, To wash us all clean;

And low knelt the shep-herds To wor-ship Him there.
"Of such is my king-dom, Per-mit them!" He said.
He'll fit us for heav-en, And there take us in.

No. 35. How Can I But Love Him?

"We love Him because He first loved us." —I JOHN iv. 19.

J. E. RANKIN, D. D.   E. S. LORENZ.

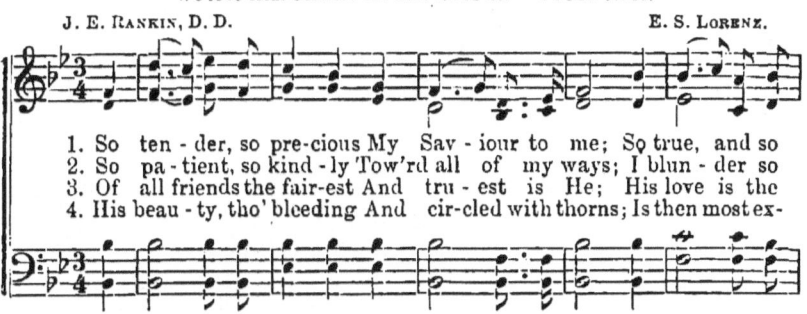

1. So ten - der, so pre-cious My Sav - iour to me; So true, and so
2. So pa - tient, so kind - ly Tow'rd all of my ways; I blun - der so
3. Of all friends the fair-est And tru - est is He; His love is the
4. His beau - ty, tho' bleeding And cir-cled with thorns; Is then most ex-

Refrain.

gra-cious, I've found Him to be.   How can I but love Him? But
blind - ly, He love still re - pays.   How, etc.
rar - est, That ev - er can be.   How, etc.
ceed - ing: For grief Him a-dorns.   How, etc.

love Him, but love Him? There's no friend above Him, poor sinner, for thee.

No, 36, Bethany, 6s & 4s, Key G,

1. Nearer, my God, to Thee,
   Nearer to Thee!
   E'en though it be a cross,
   That raiseth me;
   Still all my song shall be,
   Nearer, my God, to Thee,
   Nearer to Thee!

2. There let my way appear
   Steps up to Heaven;
   All that Thou sendest me
   In mercy given;
   Angels to beckon me
   Nearer, my God, to Thee,
   Nearer to Thee!

S. F. ADAMS.

No. 37. Sweet Canaan Land.

"A land flowing with milk and honey."—Josh. v. 6.

J. E. RANKIN, D. D.   J. E. RANKIN.

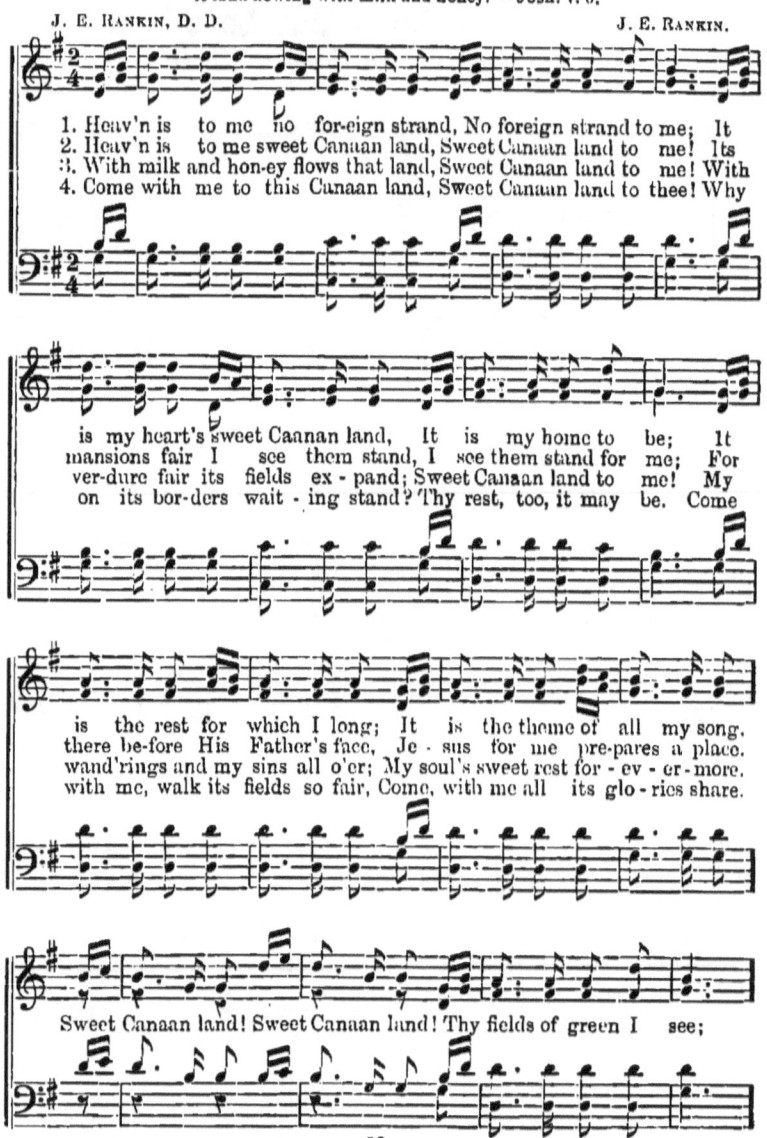

1. Heav'n is to me no for-eign strand, No foreign strand to me; It
2. Heav'n is to me sweet Canaan land, Sweet Canaan land to me! Its
3. With milk and hon-ey flows that land, Sweet Canaan land to me! With
4. Come with me to this Canaan land, Sweet Canaan land to thee! Why

is my heart's sweet Canaan land, It is my home to be; It
mansions fair I see them stand, I see them stand for me; For
ver-dure fair its fields ex - pand; Sweet Canaan land to me! My
on its bor-ders wait - ing stand? Thy rest, too, it may be. Come

is the rest for which I long; It is the theme of all my song.
there be-fore His Father's face, Je - sus for me pre-pares a place.
wand'rings and my sins all o'er; My soul's sweet rest for - ev - er - more.
with me, walk its fields so fair, Come, with me all its glo - ries share.

Sweet Canaan land! Sweet Canaan land! Thy fields of green I see;

Sweet Canaan Land--Concluded.

Sweet Canaan land! Sweet Canaan land! What can divide from thee.

No. 38. Shining Shore. 8s & 7s.

1. My days are gliding swiftly by,
And I, a pilgrim stranger,
Would not detain them as they fly,
Those hours of toil and danger.
Cho.—For now we stand on Jordan's
strand,
Our friends are passing over;
And just before, the shining shore
We may almost discover.

2. Should coming days be dark and cold,
We will not yield to sorrow,
For hope will sing, with courage bold,
"There's glory on the morrow."

3. Let sorrow's rudest tempest blow,
Each chord on earth to sever;
Our King says Come, and there's
our home,
Forever! oh, forever!
Rev. DAVID NELSON.

No. 39. Dennis. S. M.

1. Blest be the tie that binds
Our hearts in Christian love;
The fellowship of kindred minds
Is like to that above.

2. Before our Father's throne
We pour our ardent prayers;
Our fears, our hopes, our aims are one,
Our comforts and our cares.

3. We share our mutual woes,
Our mutual burdens bear;
And often for each other flows
The sympathizing tear.
Rev. JOHN FAWCETT.

No. 40. Come, Ye Disconsolate. 11s & 10s.

1. Come, ye disconsolate, where'er ye
languish, [kneel!
Come to the mercy-seat, fervently
Here bring your wounded hearts,
here tell your anguish,
Earth has no sorrow that heaven
cannot heal.

2. Joy of the desolate, light of the stray-
ing,
Hope of the penitent, fadeless and
pure, [saying,
Here speaks the Comforter, tenderly
Earth has no sorrow that heaven
cannot cure.

3. Here see the bread of life; see waters
flowing [from above;
Forth from the throne of God, pure
Come to the feast of love; come ever
knowing [can remove.
Earth has no sorrow but heaven

No. 41. To-Day. 6s & 4s.

1. To-day the Saviour calls!
Ye wanderers, come;
Oh, ye benighted souls,
Why longer roam?

2. To-day the Saviour calls!
For refuge fly;
The storm of justice falls,
And death is nigh.

3. The Spirit calls to-day!
Yield to His power;
Oh, grieve Him not away;
'Tis mercy's hour.
Rev. S. F. SMITH

No. 42. Nearer to Thee.

"Draw me, and I will run after thee."—CANT. i. 14.

J. E. RANKIN, D. D.   Lambilotte, arr. by E. S. L.

Chorus.

Nearer to Thee, my Jesus, oh, draw me! Nearer, oh, draw my spirit to Thine:

In-fin-ite love, oh, let it o'erawe me, Kindle my soul to flame divine.

1. Strange to me, that I should share, With all saints, thy wondrous care;
2. I am of-ten tost with doubt, Fears with-in, and foes with-out,
3. When blest Master, when shall I Have the peace for which I sigh?
4. Car-ry on thy work within, Help me mas-ter in-bred sin;
4. Then, blest Master, by Thy grace, Let me see Thee, face to face!

Strange, my feet, which went astray, Thou shouldst teach the narrow way.
And I oft-en blush with shame, That I love no more thy name.
When shall have thy low-ly mind? In my soul, thine im-age find?
Help me ev-er keep in view, What Thou hast for me to do.
Changed from grace to glo-ry be. And be whol-ly lost in Thee.

Not Half Has Ever Been Told--Concluded.

No. 46. Triumph By and By.

"I press toward the mark."—PHIL. iii. 14.

Dr. C. R. BLACKALL. 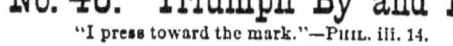 H. R. PALMER, by per.

1. The prize is set be-fore us, To win, His words implore us, The
eye of God is o'er us From on high, from on high;
His lov-ing tones are call-ing While sin is dark, ap-pall-ing.
'Tis Je-sus gen-tly call-ing, He is nigh, He is nigh.

2. We'll fol-low where He lead-eth, We'll pasture where He feedeth, We'll
yield to Him who plead-eth From on high, from on high;
Then naught from Him shall sever, Our hope shall bright-en ev - er,
And Faith shall fail us nev-er, He is nigh, He is nigh.

3. Our home is bright a - bove us, No tri - als dark to move us, But
Je - sus dear to love us There on high, there on high;
We'll give Him best en-deav-or. And praise His name for-ev-er,
His pre-cious words can nev - er, Nev-er die, nev - er die.

Triumph By and By--Concluded.

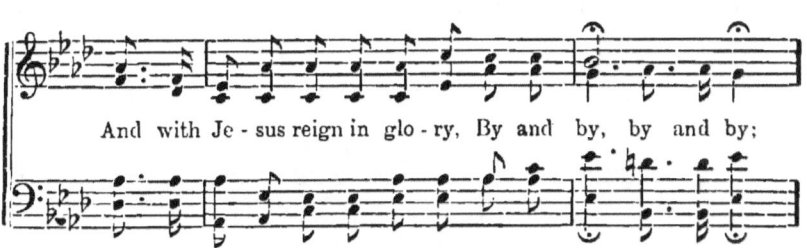
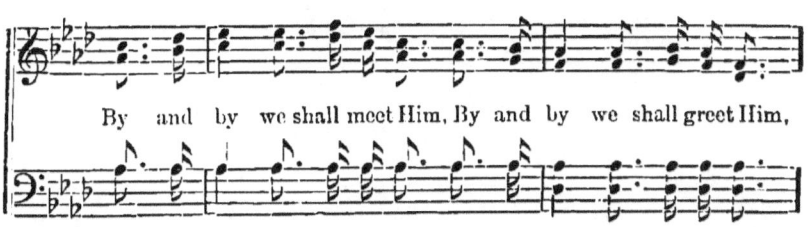
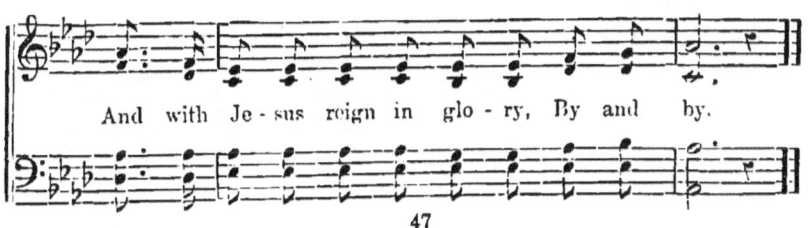

No. 47. The First Christmas Below.

"Lo, the angel of the Lord came upon them."—LUKE ii. 9.

R. E. JEREMY.   M. SAMUELS.

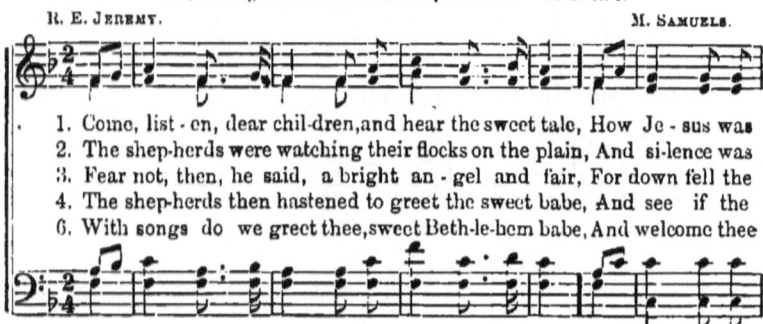

1. Come, list-en, dear chil-dren, and hear the sweet tale, How Je-sus was
2. The shep-herds were watching their flocks on the plain, And si-lence was
3. Fear not, then, he said, a bright an-gel and fair, For down fell the
4. The shep-herds then hastened to greet the sweet babe, And see if the
6. With songs do we greet thee, sweet Beth-le-hem babe, And welcome thee

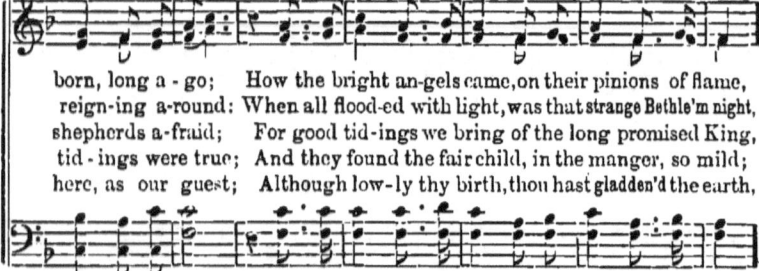

born, long a-go; How the bright an-gels came, on their pinions of flame,
reign-ing a-round; When all flood-ed with light, was that strange Bethle'm night,
shepherds a-fraid; For good tid-ings we bring of the long promised King,
tid-ings were true; And they found the fair child, in the manger, so mild;
here, as our guest; Although low-ly thy birth, thou hast gladden'd the earth,

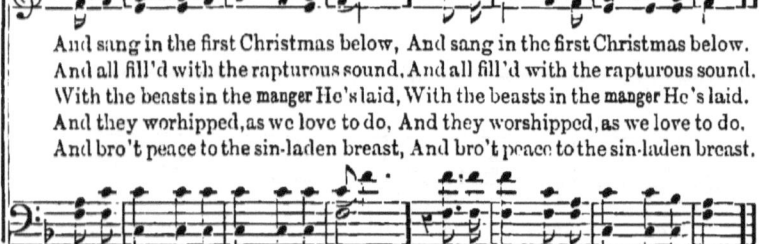

And sang in the first Christmas below, And sang in the first Christmas below.
And all fill'd with the rapturous sound, And all fill'd with the rapturous sound.
With the beasts in the manger He's laid, With the beasts in the manger He's laid.
And they worhipped, as we love to do, And they worshipped, as we love to do.
And bro't peace to the sin-laden breast, And bro't peace to the sin-laden breast.

No. 49. Fair Freedom's Land.

"A land flowing with milk and honey."—Ex. iii. 8.

J. E. RANKIN, D. D. KARL REDEN.

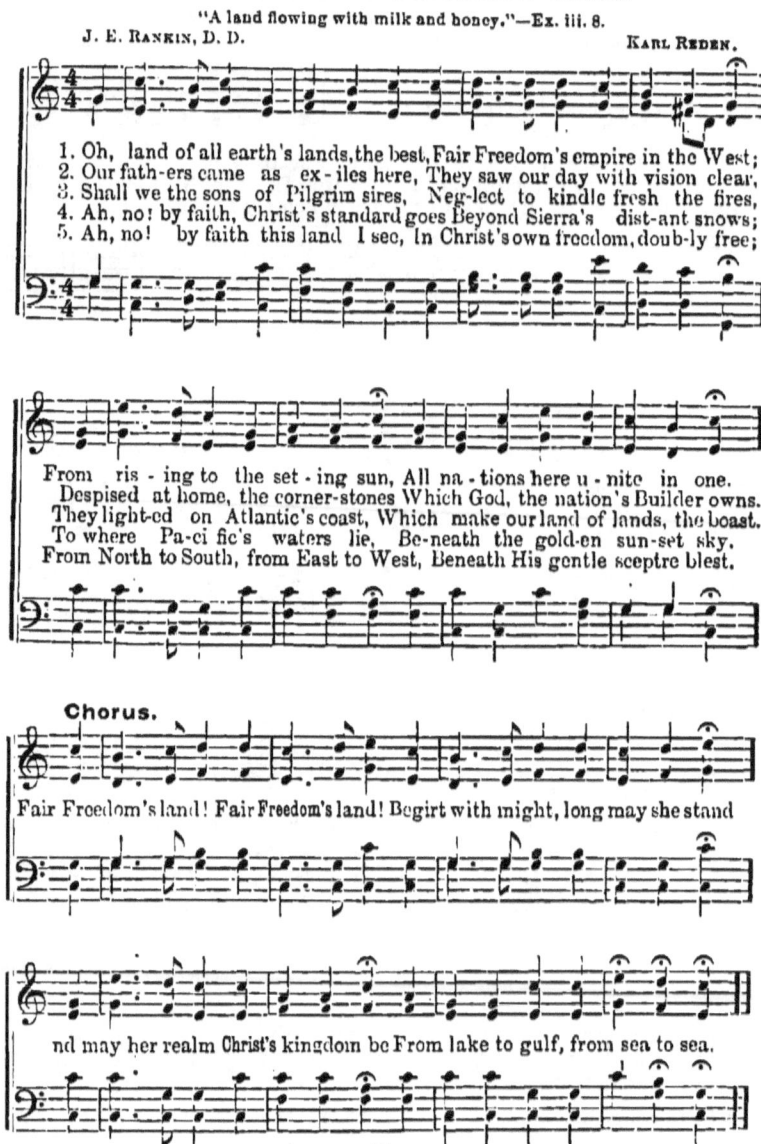

1. Oh, land of all earth's lands, the best, Fair Freedom's empire in the West;
2. Our fath-ers came as ex-iles here, They saw our day with vision clear,
3. Shall we the sons of Pilgrim sires, Neg-lect to kindle fresh the fires,
4. Ah, no! by faith, Christ's standard goes Beyond Sierra's dist-ant snows;
5. Ah, no! by faith this land I see, In Christ's own freedom, doub-ly free;

From ris-ing to the set-ing sun, All na-tions here u-nite in one.
Despised at home, the corner-stones Which God, the nation's Builder owns.
They light-ed on Atlantic's coast, Which make our land of lands, the boast.
To where Pa-ci fic's waters lie, Be-neath the gold-en sun-set sky.
From North to South, from East to West, Beneath His gentle sceptre blest.

Chorus.

Fair Freedom's land! Fair Freedom's land! Begirt with might, long may she stand

nd may her realm Christ's kingdom be From lake to gulf, from sea to sea.

No. 51. I'm Redeemed, Bought with a Price.

"Not redeemed with corruptible things, but with the precious blood of Christ."—
1 Pet. i. 18, 19.

R. N. Walters. L. S. Edwards.

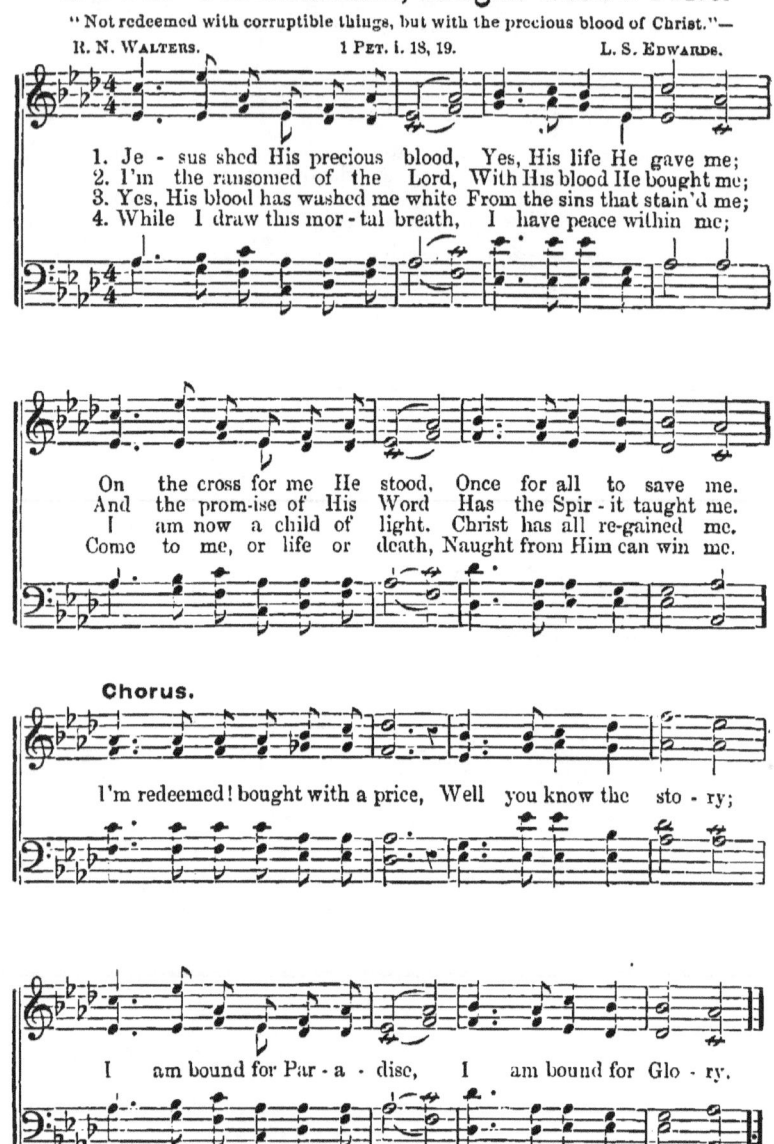

1. Je - sus shed His precious blood, Yes, His life He gave me;
2. I'm the ransomed of the Lord, With His blood He bought me;
3. Yes, His blood has washed me white From the sins that stain'd me;
4. While I draw this mor - tal breath, I have peace within me;

On the cross for me He stood, Once for all to save me.
And the prom-ise of His Word Has the Spir - it taught me.
I am now a child of light. Christ has all re-gained me.
Come to me, or life or death, Naught from Him can win me.

Chorus.

I'm redeemed! bought with a price, Well you know the sto - ry;
I am bound for Par - a - dise, I am bound for Glo - ry.

No. 54. Behold, How Sweet.

"Behold my servant, whom I uphold."—Is. xlii. 1.

J. E. RANKIN, D. D.   Rev. S. MORRISON.

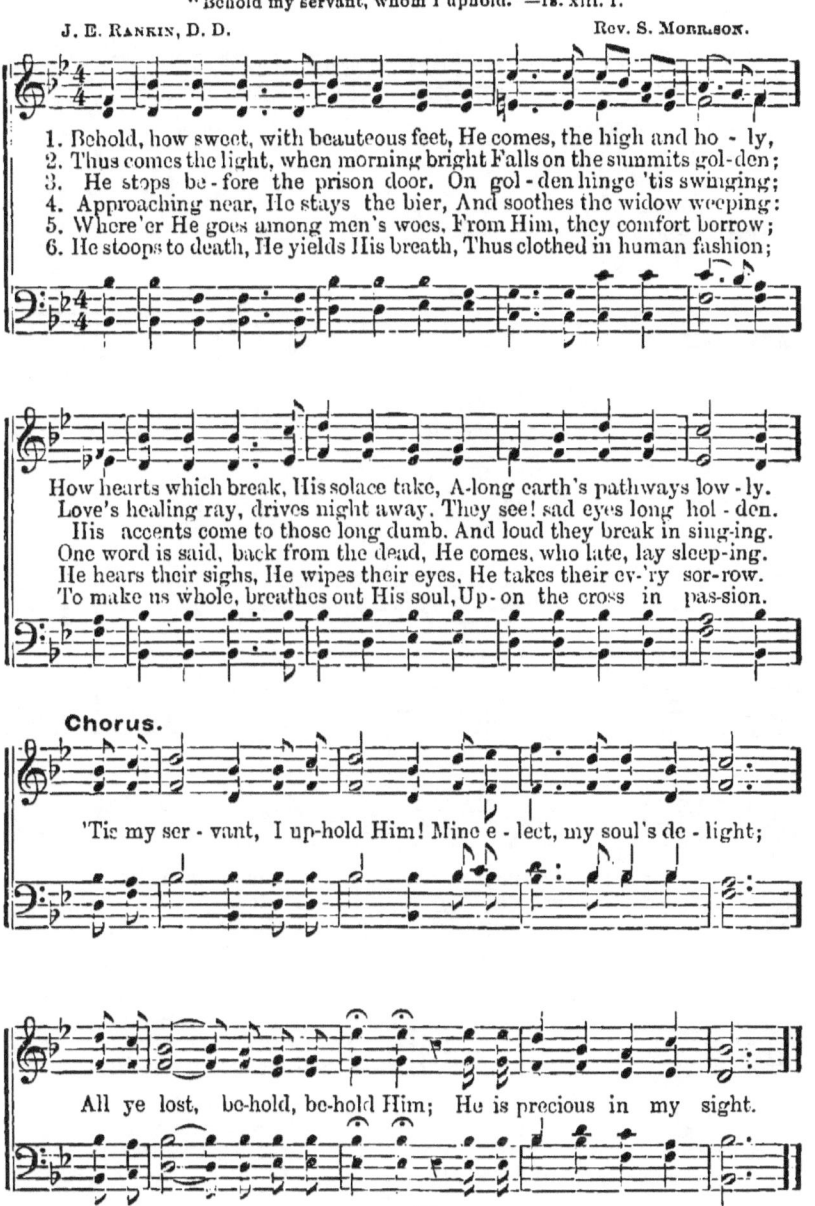

1. Behold, how sweet, with beauteous feet, He comes, the high and ho-ly,
2. Thus comes the light, when morning bright Falls on the summits gol-den;
3. He stops be-fore the prison door. On gol-den hinge 'tis swinging;
4. Approaching near, He stays the bier, And soothes the widow weeping:
5. Where'er He goes among men's woes, From Him, they comfort borrow;
6. He stoops to death, He yields His breath, Thus clothed in human fashion;

How hearts which break, His solace take, A-long earth's pathways low-ly.
Love's healing ray, drives night away. They see! sad eyes long hol-den.
His accents come to those long dumb. And loud they break in sing-ing.
One word is said, back from the dead, He comes, who late, lay sleep-ing.
He hears their sighs, He wipes their eyes, He takes their ev-'ry sor-row.
To make us whole, breathes out His soul, Up-on the cross in pas-sion.

Chorus.

'Tis my ser-vant, I up-hold Him! Mine e-lect, my soul's de-light;

All ye lost, be-hold, be-hold Him; He is precious in my sight.

No. 55. Blessed Jesus.

"Unto you therefore which believe he is precious."—1 Pet. ii. 7

O. F. P.
Otis F. Presbrey.

Cheerfully.

1. O how hap-py I should be, Je-sus loves and cares for me;
2. When my heart is lone and sad, Thy sure prom-ise makes me glad;
3. When this fleeting life is o'er, I will sing on yon-der shore;

Ev-er hears me when I pray, Lis-tens to each word I say.
Thou wilt light-en ev-'ry task, Al-ways help when-e'er I ask.
Bless-ed Je-sus, I shall be Hap-py thro' e-ter-ni-ty.

Chorus.

Bless-ed Je-sus, 'twas for me, Thou did'st suf-fer on the tree;
Pre-cious Sav-iour, may I be, Dai-ly more and more like Thee?

No. 56. Hebron. L. M.

1. Jesus, and shall it ever be,
   A mortal man ashamed of Thee!
   Ashamed of Thee, whom angels praise,
   Whose glories shine thro' endless days?

2. Ashamed of Jesus! that dear Friend
   On whom my hopes of heaven depend?
   No! when I blush, be this my shame,
   That I no more revere His name.

3. Ashamed of Jesus! yes, I may
   When I've no guilt to wash away;
   No tear to wipe, no good to crave,
   No fear to quell, no soul to save.

No. 58. There's a Better Time A-Coming.

"In the fear of the Lord is strong confidence."—Prov. xiv, 26.

Words and Music by J. E. Rankin, D. D.   Arr. by J. W. Bischoff.

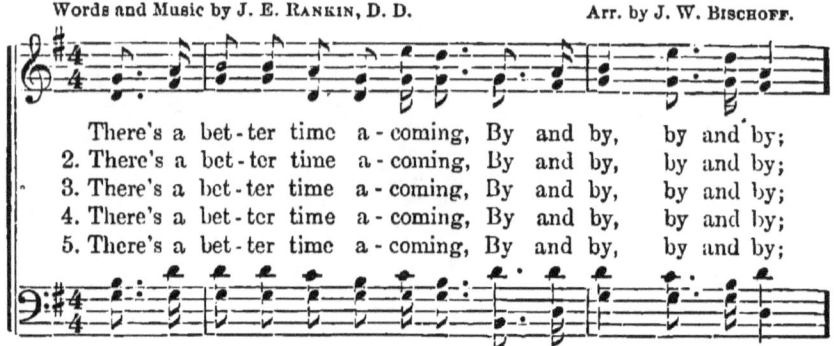

There's a bet-ter time a-coming, By and by, by and by;
2. There's a bet-ter time a-coming, By and by, by and by;
3. There's a bet-ter time a-coming, By and by, by and by;
4. There's a bet-ter time a-coming, By and by, by and by;
5. There's a bet-ter time a-coming, By and by, by and by;

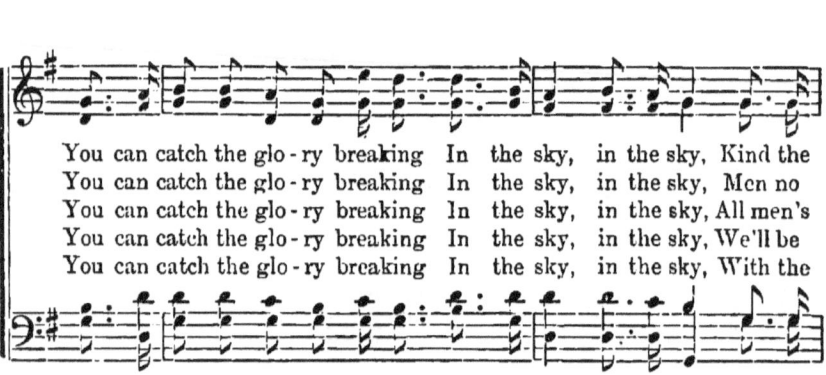

You can catch the glo-ry breaking In the sky, in the sky, Kind the
You can catch the glo-ry breaking In the sky, in the sky, Men no
You can catch the glo-ry breaking In the sky, in the sky, All men's
You can catch the glo-ry breaking In the sky, in the sky, We'll be
You can catch the glo-ry breaking In the sky, in the sky, With the

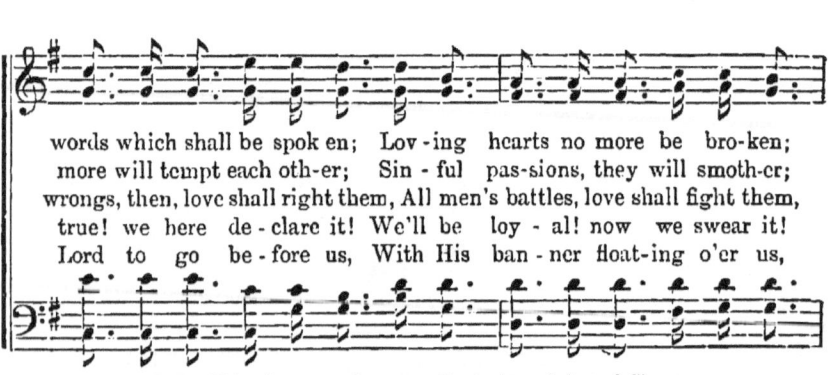

words which shall be spok en; Lov-ing hearts no more be bro-ken;
more will tempt each oth-er; Sin-ful pas-sions, they will smoth-er;
wrongs, then, love shall right them, All men's battles, love shall fight them,
true! we here de-clare it! We'll be loy-al! now we swear it!
Lord to go be-fore us, With His ban-ner float-ing o'er us,

N. B.—This piece may be sung effectively as Solo and Chorus.

There's a Better Time A-Coming—Concluded.

The King Who is Greatest--Concluded.

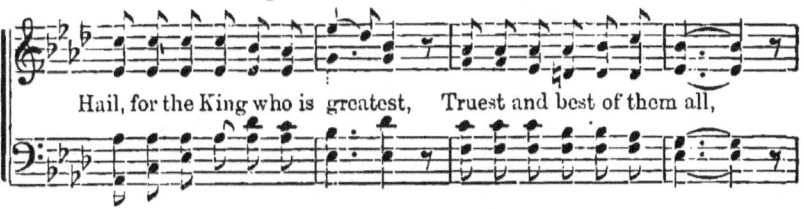

Hail, for the King who is greatest, Truest and best of them all,

He will attend when His weak ones Lovingly, trustingly call,

He will attend when His weak ones Lovingly, trustingly call.

No. 60. Martyn. 7s, D.

1. Jesus, lover of my soul,
   Let me to thy bosom fly,
   While the nearer waters roll,
   While the tempest still is high.
   Hide me, O my Saviour, hide,
   Till the storm of life is past;
   Safe into the haven guide,
   Oh, receive my soul at last.

2. Other refuge have I none;
   Hangs my helpless soul on thee;
   Leave, oh, leave me not alone;
   Still support and comfort me.
4. All my trust on thee is stayed;
   All my help from thee I bring:
   Cover my defenceless head
   With the shadow of thy wing.

No. 61. Work. 7s & 6s.

1. Work, for the night is coming;
   Work through the morning hours;
   Work, while the dew is sparkling;
   Work, 'mid springing flowers;
   Work, when the day grows brighter,
   Work, in the glowing sun;
   Work, for the night is coming,
   When man's work is done.

2. Work, for the night is coming;
   Work through the sunny noon;
   Fill brightest hours with labor;
   Rest comes sure and soon.
   Give every flying minute
   Something to keep in store;
   Work, for the night is coming,
   When man works no more

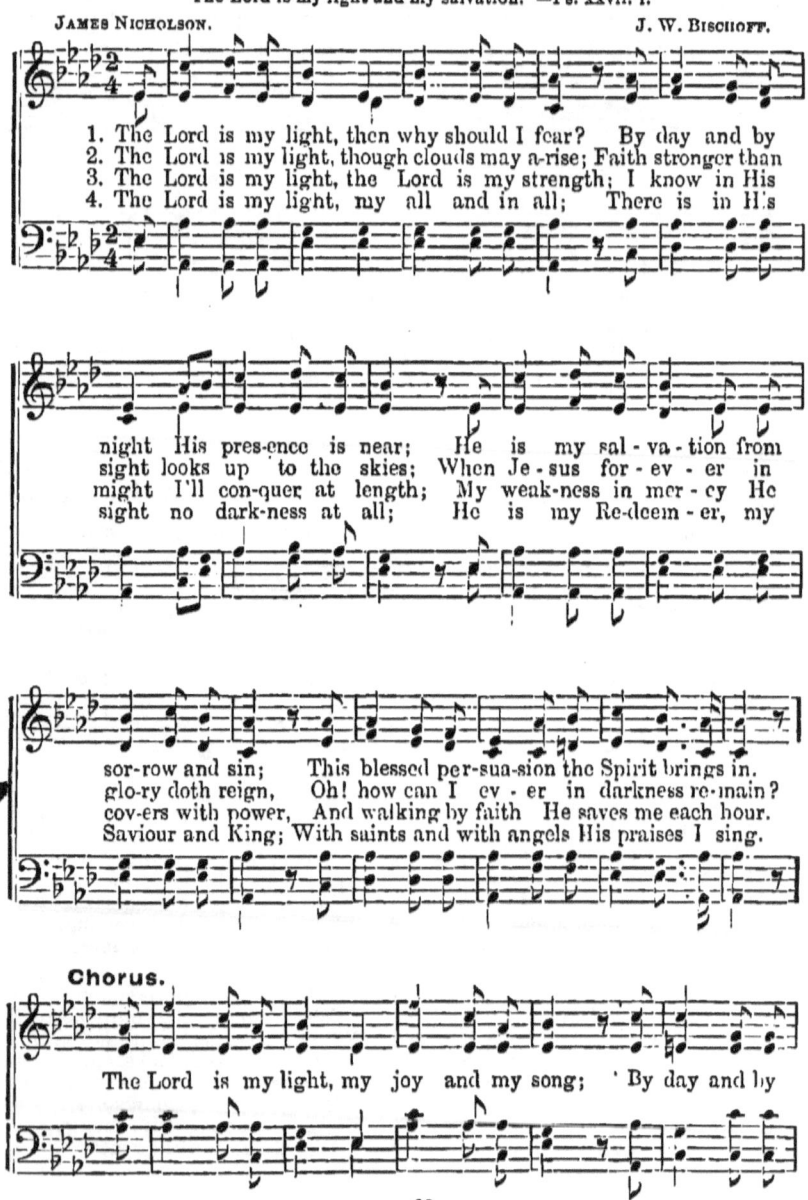

The Lord is My Light—Concluded.

night He leads me a-long: The Lord is my light, my

joy and my song; By day and by night He leads me a-long.

No. 63. Come, Trembling Soul.

"Be not afraid, only believe."—MARK. v, 36.

J. W. BISCHOFF, by per.

1. Come, trembling soul, be not a - fraid; On Jesus all thy sins were laid;
2. The Suff'rer in the gar-den see, The Lamb of God on Cal-va-ry;
3. The crimson stream, thy Saviour's blood, Has pow'r to bring thee nigh to God;

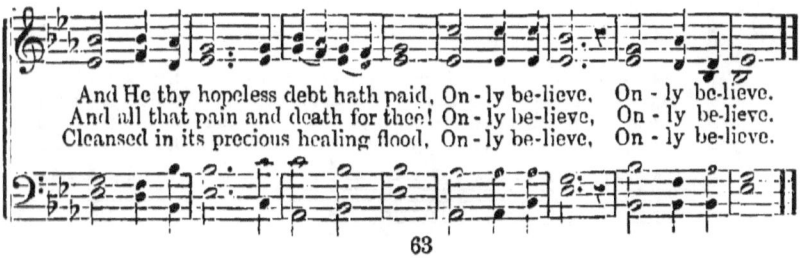

And He thy hopeless debt hath paid, On - ly be-lieve, On - ly be-lieve.
And all that pain and death for thee! On - ly be-lieve, On - ly be-lieve.
Cleansed in its precious healing flood, On - ly be-lieve, On - ly be-lieve.

No. 64. The Gospel Bells.

For God so loved the world, that he gave his only begotten Son. —JOHN, 3:16.

S. WESLEY MARTIN. S. W. M.

1. The Gos-pel bells are ring-ing, O-ver land, from sea to sea; Bless-ed news of free sal-va-tion Do they of-fer you and me.
2. The Gos-pel bells in-vite us To a feast pre-pared for all; Do not slight the in-vi-ta-tion, Nor re-ject the gra-cious call,
3. The Gos-pel bells give warn-ing, As they sound from day to day, Of the fate which doth a-wait them Who for-ev-er will de-lay.
4. The Gos-pel bells are joy-ful, As they ech-o far and wide, Bear-ing notes of per-fect par-don, Thro' a Sav-iour cru-ci-fied.

"For God so loved the world That His on-ly Son He gave, Who-so-e'er be-liev-eth in Him Ev-er-last-ing life shall have."
"I am the bread of life; Eat of me, thou hun-gry soul, Tho' your sins be red as crim-son, They shall be as white as wool."
"Es-cape thou, for thy life; Tar-ry not in all the plain, Nor be-hind thee look, oh, nev-er, Lest thou be con-sumed in pain."
"Good tid-ings of great joy To all peo-ple do I bring, Un-to you is born a Sav-iour, Which is Christ the Lord" and King.

The Gospel Bells--Concluded.

Chorus.

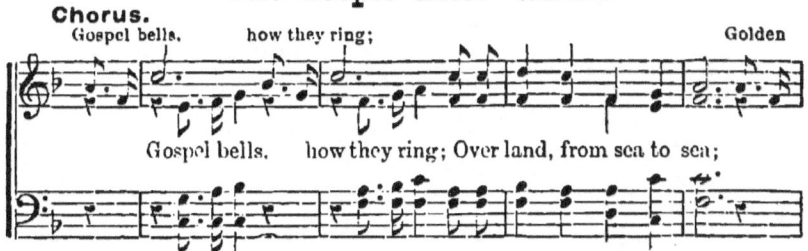

Gospel bells, how they ring; Over land, from sea to sea;

Golden bells free-ly bring Blessed news to you and me.

No. 65, Shall We Gather.

1. Shall we gather at the river,
   Where bright angel feet have trod,
   With its crystal tide forever
   Flowing by the throne of God?
Cho.—Yes we'll gather at the river,
   The beautiful, the beautiful river,
   Gather with the saints at the river
   That flows by the throne of God.

2. On the margin of the river,
   Washing up its silver spray,
   We will walk and worship ever,
   All the happy golden day.

3. Ere we reach the shining river,
   Lay we every burden down;
   Grace our spirits will deliver,
   And provide a robe and crown.

4. Soon we'll reach the shining river,
   Soon our pilgrimage will cease;
   Soon our happy hearts will quiver
   With the melody of peace.
   R. Lowry.

No. 66, The Happy Land.

1. There is a happy land,
     Far, far away;
   Where saints in glory stand,
     Bright, bright as day.
   Oh, how they sweetly sing,
   Worthy is our Saviour King,
   Loud let His praises ring,
     Praise, praise for aye.

2. Come to that happy land,
     Come, come away;
   Why will ye doubting stand,
     Why still delay?
   Oh, we shall happy be
   When from sin and sorrow free!
   Lord we shall live with Thee,
     Blest, blest for aye.

3. Bright, in that happy land,
     Beams every eye;
   Kept by a Father's hand,
     Love cannot die.
   Oh, then, to glory run,
   Be a crown and kingdom won;
   And bright above the sun
     We'll reign for aye.

I Long to be There--Concluded

groves of that country so fair, There the bright angels stand. Ever-

more in that land, I long, oh, I long to be there.

No. 68. Ariel. C. P. M.

1. Oh, could I speak the matchless worth,
Oh, could I sound the glories forth
Which in my Saviour shine!
I'd soar and touch the heavenly strings,
And vie with Gabriel, while he sings
‖: In notes almost divine. :‖

2. I'd sing the precious blood he spilt,
My ransom from the dreadful guilt
Of sin and wrath divine;
I'd sing his glorious righteousness,
In which all-perfect heavenly dress
‖: My soul shall ever shine. :‖

3. I'd sing the character he bears,
And all the forms of love he wears,
Exalted on his throne:
In loftiest songs of sweetest praise,
I would to everlasting days
‖: Make all his glories known. :‖

4. Soon the delightful day will come
When my dear Lord shall bring me home,
And I shall see his face:
Then with my Saviour, brother, friend,
A blest eternity I'll spend.
‖: Triumphant in his grace. :‖

MEDLEY.

No. 69. Frederic

1. I would not live alway; I ask not to stay
Where storm after storm rises dark o'er the way.
The few lurid mornings that dawn on us here
Are enough for life's woes, full enough for its cheer.

2. Who, who would live alway, away from his God,
Away from yon heaven, that blissful abode,
Where rivers of pleasure flow o'er the bright plains,
And the noontide of glory eternally reigns?

3. Where the saints of all ages in harmony meet,
Their Saviour and brethren transported to greet;
While anthems of rapture unceasingly roll,
And the smile of the Lord is the feast of the soul.

MUHLENBURGH.

No. 70. He Careth for You.

"Casting your care on Him; for He careth for you."—1 Pet. v. 7.

James Nicholson.   J. H. Tenney.

1. Be-liev-er in Je-sus, wher-ev-er you are, When sor-rows se-vere o-ver-whelm you with care, Re-mem-ber that Je-sus is faith-ful and true, Cast your care upon Him, for He car-eth for you.
2. When-e'er you are tempted, and burden'd with fear, Take courage, for Je-sus your Saviour is near; And though overwhelmed, as life's sins you re-view, Cast your care upon Him, for He car-eth for you.
3. When loved ones are tak-en a-way from your side, And summoned to glo-ry, with Christ to a-bide. When sad, that earth's friendships you can-not re-new; Cast your care upon Him, for He car-eth for you.
4. Though Providence nothing but trouble should send, And you've been be-trayed by a treacherous friend; Though foes, without mer-cy, your life should pursue, Cast your care upon Him, for He car-eth for you.
5. Hold fast to your confidence, Christian, hold fast, For though among li-ons your soul should be cast, The God, who saved Daniel, shall keep you in view, Cast your care upon Him, for He car-eth for you.

Chorus.

He car-eth for you, and He car-eth for me, To trust Him for-

He Careth for You--Concluded.

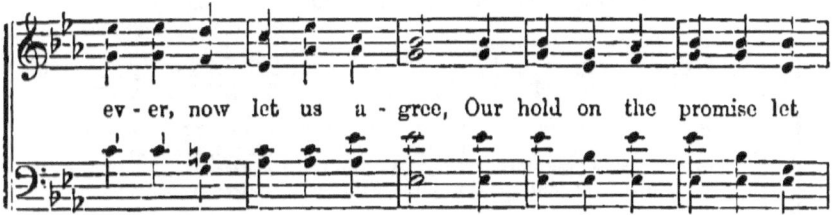

ev-er, now let us a-gree, Our hold on the promise let

noth-ing un-do, Cast your care upon Him, For He car-eth for you.

No. 71. What a Friend.

1. What a friend we have in Jesus,
All our sins and griefs to bear;
What a privilege to carry
Every thing to God in prayer.
Oh, what peace we often forfeit!
Oh, what needless pain we bear!
All because we do not carry
Every thing to God in prayer.

2. Have we trials and temptations?
Is there trouble anywhere?
We should never be discouraged;
Take it to the Lord in prayer.
Can we find a Friend so faithful,
Who will all our sorrows share?
Jesus knows our every weakness;
Take it to the Lord in prayer.

3. Are we weak and heavy laden,
Cumbered with a load of care?
Precious Saviour, still our refuge,
Take it to the Lord in prayer.
Do thy friends despise, forsake thee?
Take it to the Lord in prayer;
In his arms he'll take and shield thee;
Thou wilt find a solace there.
Rev. H. Bonar, D. D.

No. 72. Lebanon. S. M. D.

1. I was a wandering sheep;
I did not love the fold;
I did not love my Shepherd's voice,
I would not be controlled.
I was a wayward child;
I did not love my home;
I did not love my Father's voice;
I loved afar to roam.

2. The Shepherd sought his sheep.
The Father sought his child;
They followed me o'er vale and hill.
O'er deserts waste and wild.
They found me nigh to death,
Famished, and faint, and lone;
They bound me with the bands of love,
They saved the wandering one.

3. Jesus my shepherd is;
"Twas He that loved my soul;
'Twas he that washed me in his blood,
"Twas he that made me whole;
'Twas he that sought the lost,
That found the wandering sheep,
'Twas he that brought me to the fold,
'Tis he that still doth keep.
Dr. H. Bonar.

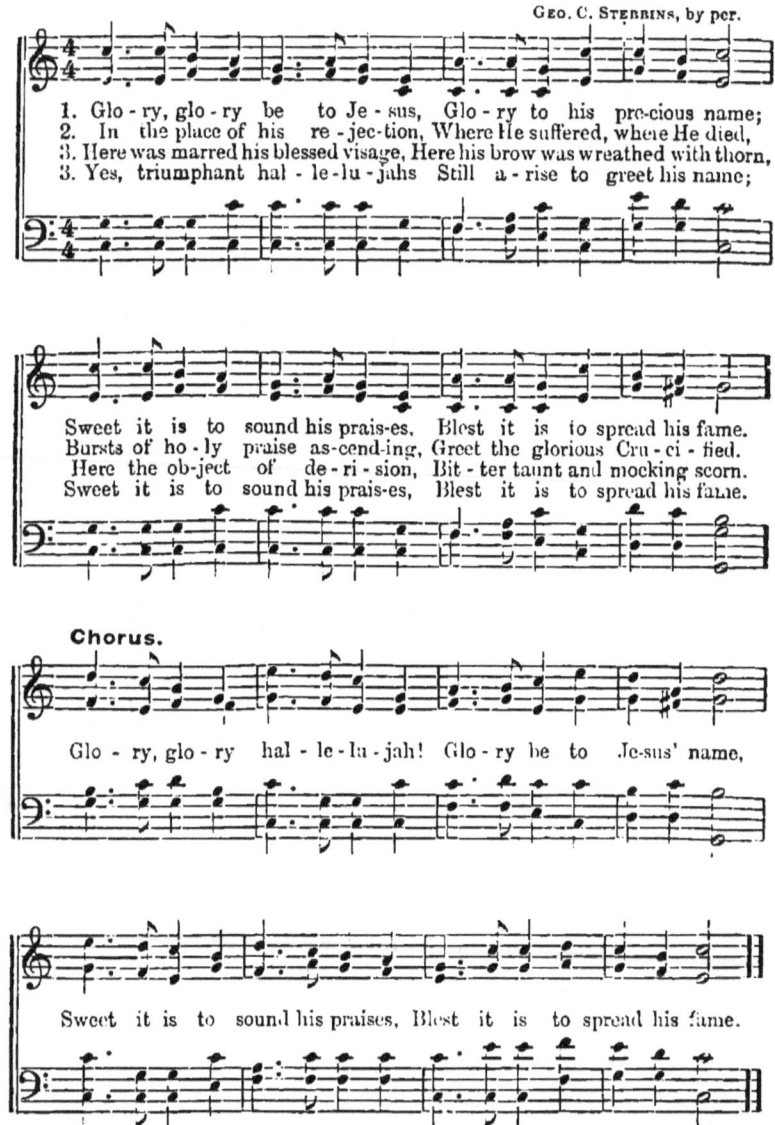

No. 74. When I Walk Thro' the Valley.

"Though I walk through the valley of the shadow of death, I will fear no evil."—Ps. xxiii. 4.

J. E. RANKIN, D. D.　　　　　　　　　　　　　　　　　　　　J. E. RANKIN.

1. When I walk through the valley of death, When I yield up to Jes-us my
2. I will lean my poor head on His breast, I will sleep the sweet sleep of the
3. I will come, come again, if I go, And the place and the way well ye

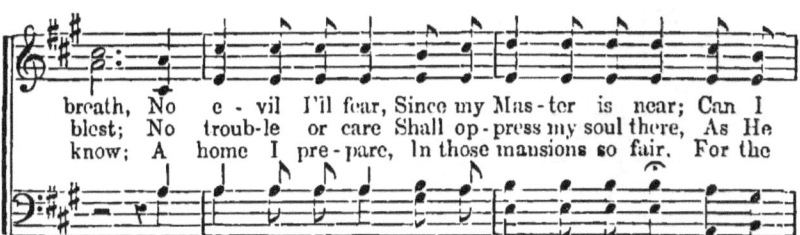

breath, No e-vil I'll fear, Since my Mas-ter is near; Can I
blest; No troub-le or care Shall op-press my soul there, As He
know; A home I pre-pare, In those mansions so fair. For the

Refrain.

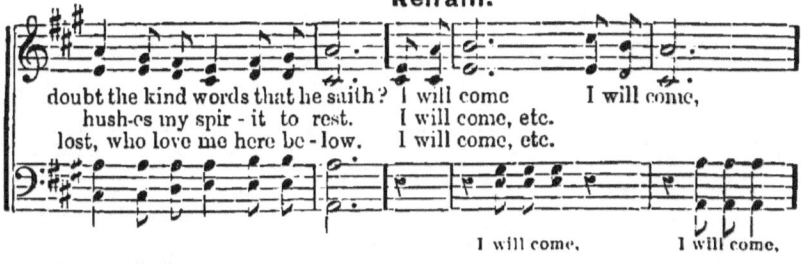

doubt the kind words that he saith?　I will come　　I will come,
hush-es my spir-it to rest.　　　I will come, etc.
lost, who love me here be-low.　　I will come, etc.

I will come,　　I will come,

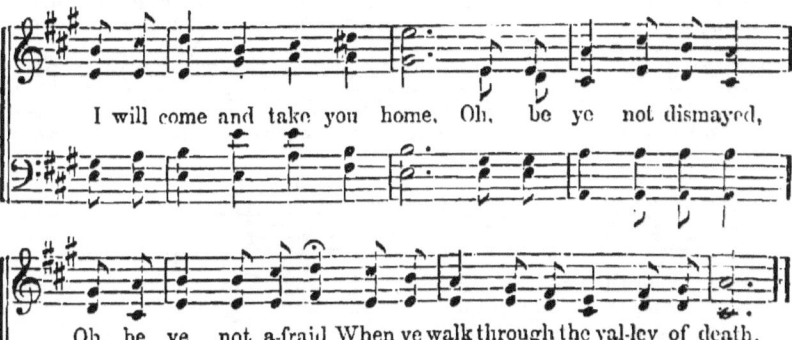

I will come and take you home. Oh, be ye not dismayed,
Oh, be ye not a-fraid When ye walk through the val-ley of death.

The King's Highway—Concluded.

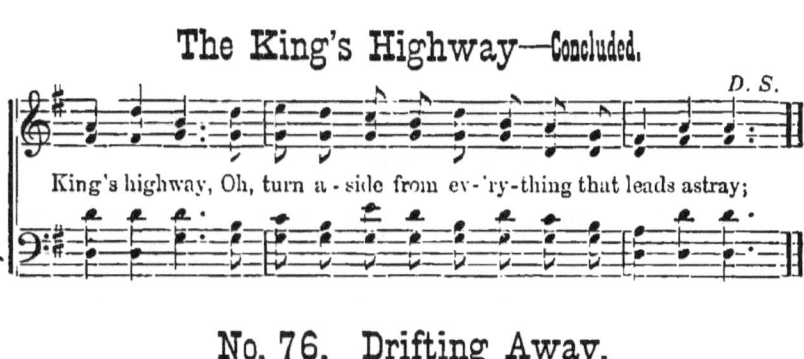

King's highway, Oh, turn a-side from ev-'ry-thing that leads astray;

No. 76. Drifting Away.

"Every one of them is gone back; they are altogether become filthy; there is none that doeth good, no, not one."—Ps. liii. 3.

E. A. BARNES. A. J. ABBEY, by per.

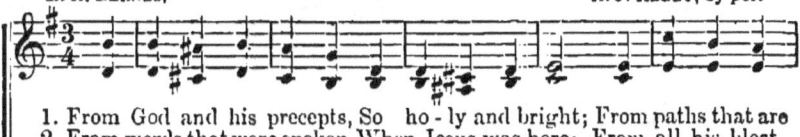

1. From God and his precepts, So ho-ly and bright; From paths that are
2. From words that were spoken When Jesus was here; From all his blest
3. From grace that is wait-ing, New prospects to give; From love that will

pleasant, Because they are right; From truths in the Bible, That all should o-
teachings, So sim-ple, yet dear; From hope in his favor, That soul charming
help you As Christians to live; From heaven's bright portals, At life's final

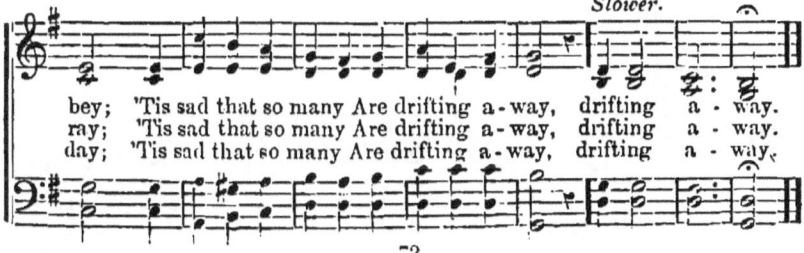

bey; 'Tis sad that so many Are drifting a-way, drifting a-way.
ray; 'Tis sad that so many Are drifting a-way, drifting a-way.
day; 'Tis sad that so many Are drifting a-way, drifting a-way.

Jesus, all the Way—Concluded.

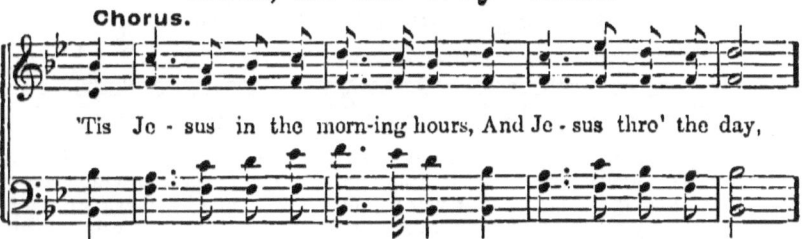

'Tis Je-sus in the morn-ing hours, And Je-sus thro' the day,

And Je-sus in life's ev-en-time, And Je-sus all the way.

No. 78. Fountain. C, M,

1. There is a fountain filled with blood
 Drawn from Immanuel's veins,
 And sinners, plung'd beneath that
 Lose all their guilty stains. [flood,
 Cho.—Lose all, etc.

2. The dying thief rejoiced to see
 That fountain in his day;
 And there may I, though vile as he,
 Wash all my sins away.
 Cho.—Wash all, etc.

3. Dear dying Lamb! thy precious blood
 Shall never lose its power,
 Till all the ransomed church of God
 Are saved to sin no more.
 Cho.—Are saved, etc.

4. E'er since by faith I saw the stream
 Thy flowing wounds supply,
 Redeeming love has been my theme,
 And shall be till I die!
 Cho.—And shall, etc.

No. 79. The Sweet Story.

1. I think, when I read that sweet story
 of old,
 When Jesus was here among men,
 How he called little children as lambs
 to his fold,
 I should like to have been with
 them then.

2. Yet still to his footstool in prayer I
 may go,
 And ask for a share in his love;
 And if I thus earnestly seek him be-
 low,
 I shall see him and hear him above.

3. In that beautiful place he has gone
 to prepare [en;
 For all who are washed and forgiv-
 And many dear children are gather-
 ing there,
 "For of such is the kingdom of
 heaven."

O Prodigal, Don't Stay Away—Concluded.

There's a kiss, kind and true, Then O prod-i-gal, don't stay a-way.

No. 81. Beyond the River.

"We shall be like him; for we shall see him as he is."—1 John iii. 2.

J. E. R. J. E. RANKIN, D. D.

1. Friends we have beyond the riv-er, Shin-ing ones that wait us there:
2. At the feet of Je-sus seat-ed, Ah! they need our pray'rs no more;
3. Names of kindred, sacred, sainted, On the wing of mem'ry brought;
4. Could they tell, oh, what the story, Of their growth from grace to grace;
5. They have on-ly gone be-fore us, Lost to sight and sense they are;

Death can reach them, never, never, In that realm so bright and fair.
Their life's con-flict all com-plet-ed, Rest they on that ra-diant shore.
By the stain of sin un-taint-ed, How they an-swer to our thought.
Of their change to great-er glo-ry, As they see the Lord's own face!
But from realms of glo-ry o'er us, We can catch their light a-far.

D. S. *Friends we have beyond the riv-er, Shining ones that wait us there.*

Refrain, D. S.

Be-yond, be-yond the riv-er. Be-yond, be-yond the riv-er,

No. 82. Falling Feathers.

A CHILD'S IDEA OF SNOW.

Blessed is he that considereth the poor.—PSALMS, 41:1.

Mrs. L. H. WASHINGTON. J. W. BISCHOFF.

1. Mam - ma, said lit - tle Nel - lie, ... May broth - er Frank and I ...... Go out and catch the feath - ers That are fall - ing from the sky? We will make them in - to pil - lows For the
2. They are cling-ing to the wil - lows O - ver lit - tle sis - ter's bed, Where you laid her in the gar - den, With the rose-bush at her head; ...... She does not need the feath - ers, Nor earth's
3. Last night, you know, you told me, When I said my bed was cold, ... That there are man-y chil-dren, ... And man-y who are old, ... Who have no nice new cloth-ing ...... To
4. And, moth - er, I re - mem - bered, ... As I grew warm in bed, All a - bout those need-y chil-dren, And I thought of what you said; And I asked our Heav'n-ly Fath - er To pro-

Falling Feathers--Concluded.

No. 86. The Wee Lambs of the Fold.

"He shall gather the lambs with His arm, and carry them in His bosom."—Is. xl. 11.

J. W. B.

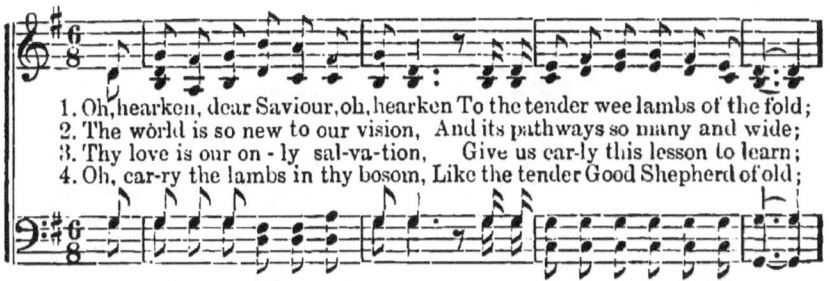

1. Oh, hearken, dear Saviour, oh, hearken To the tender wee lambs of the fold;
2. The world is so new to our vision, And its pathways so many and wide;
3. Thy love is our on-ly sal-va-tion, Give us ear-ly this lesson to learn;
4. Oh, car-ry the lambs in thy bosom, Like the tender Good Shepherd of old;

Reach out thy strong arm and protect us, Lest we wander away in the cold.
We never can tread them in safety, Blessed Saviour, unless thou wilt guide,
From sins and temptations of childhood, To its shelter, oh, help us to turn.
And guard us with care all so faithful, That no one shall be lost from Thy fold.

Chorus.

Oh, shelter the little wee lambs of the fold, Shelter them warm from the biting cold,

Shelter the lambs, shelter the lambs, The little wee lambs of the fold.

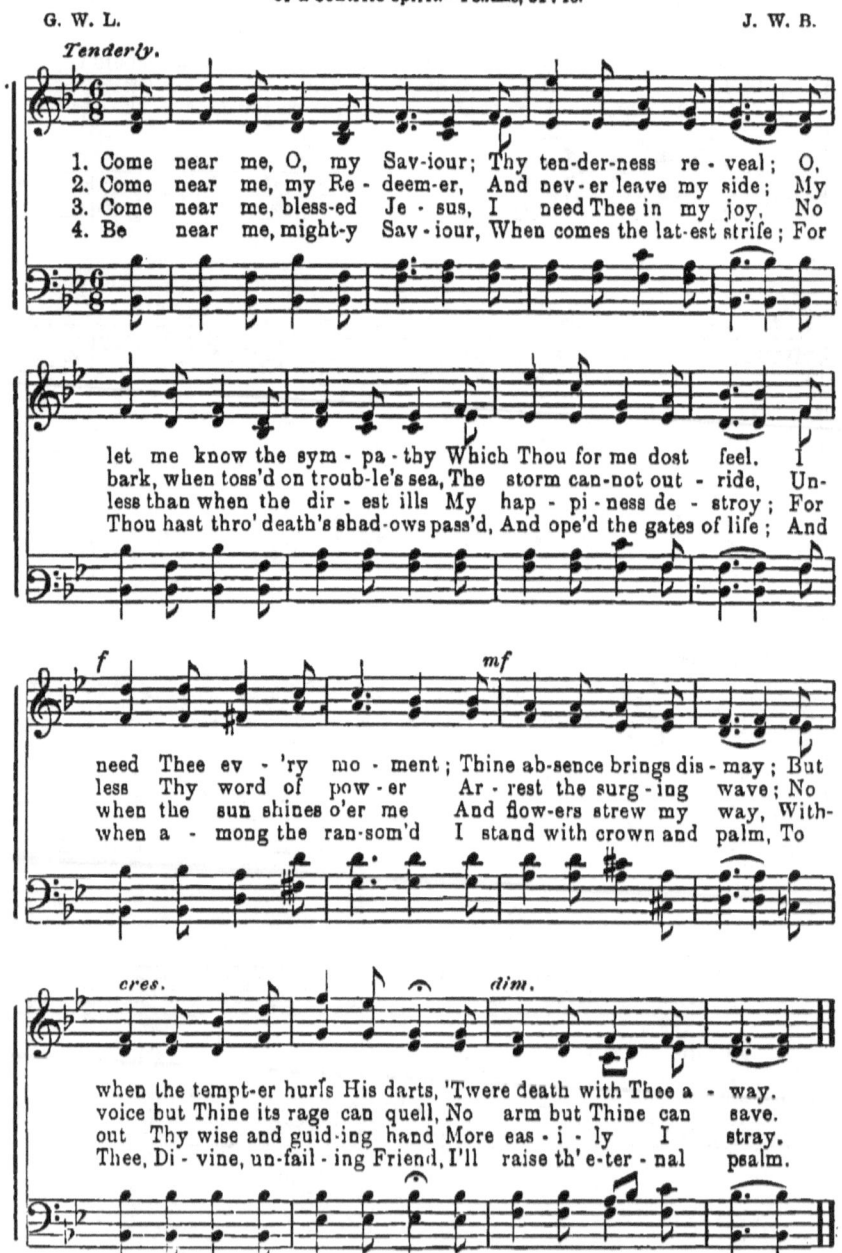

No. 91. Trusting in the Promise.

"He is faithful that promised."—HEB. x. 23.

Rev. H. B. HARTZLER.   E. S. LORENZ, by per.

1. I have found repose for my wea-ry soul, Trusting in the promise of the
2. I will sing my song as the days go by, Trusting in the promise of the
3. Oh, the peace and joy of the life I live, Trusting in the promise of the

Sav - iour; And a har - bor safe when the bil - lows roll,
Sav - iour; And re - joice in hope, while I live or die,
Sav - iour; Oh, the strength and grace on - ly God can give,

Trusting in the promise of the Saviour, I will fear no foe in the
Trusting in the promise of the Saviour, I can smile at grief, and a-
Trusting in the promise of the Saviour, Who-so-ev - er will may be

dead-ly strife, Trusting in the prom-ise of the Sav - iour; I will
bide in pain, Trusting in the prom-ise of the Sav - iour; And the
saved to - day, Trusting in the prom-ise of the Sav - iour; And be-

Trusting in the Promise--Concluded.

bear my lot in the toil of life, Trusting in the promise of the
loss of all shall be high-est gain, Trusting in, etc.
gin to walk in the ho-ly way, Trusting in, etc.

Chorus.

Sav-iour. Lean-ing on His mighty arm for-ev-er,
Nev-er from His lov-ing heart to sev-er, I will rest by grace
In His strong embrace, Trusting in the prom-ise of the Sav-iour.

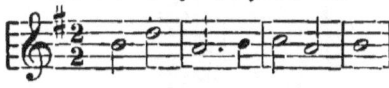

No. 92. Pleyel's Hymn. 7s.

1. Brother, hast thou wandered far
   From thy Father's happy home,
   With thyself and God at war?
   Turn thee, brother, homeward come.

2. Hast thou wasted all the powers
   God for noble uses gave?
   Squandered life's most noble hours?
   Turn thee, brother, God can save.

3. He can heal the deepest wound,
   He thy gentlest prayer can hear;
   Seek Him, for He may be found;
   Call upon Him; He is near.

   Rev. J. F. CLARKE.

No. 93. That Beautiful Land.

"In my Father's house are many mansions; if it were not so, I would have told you. I go to prepare a place for you."—JOHN xii. 2.

O. F. P.　　　　　　　　　　　　　　　　　　　　　　　　　O. F. PRESBREY.

1. There's a far a-way, beau-ti-ful land, With its man-sions so bright and so fair; And its streets with sweet breez-es are fanned; 'Tis the home of the soul o-ver there.
2. I have friends in that beau-ti-ful land, Where no sor-rows or tri-als o'er come; They will greet me when cross-ing the strand, They are wait-ing to wel-come me home.
3. I shall sing in that beau-ti-ful land The new song of re-demp-tion and love; I shall hear the sweet har-mo-ny grand, As it sweeps through those man-sions a-bove.
4. I shall rest in that beau-ti-ful land, All life's bur-dens and toils will be o'er; With my Sav-iour for-ev-er shall stand 'Mid the host on the ev-er-green shore.

Chorus.

Oh, that beau-ti-ful, beau-ti-ful land, The dear

That Beautiful Land--Concluded.

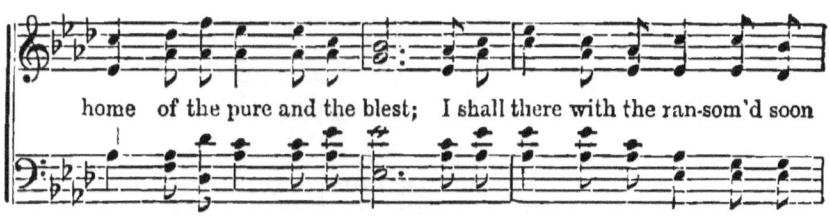

home of the pure and the blest; I shall there with the ran-som'd soon

stand, In that beau - ti - ful land I shall rest.

No. 94. Missionary Hymn. 7s & 6s.

1. From Greenland's icy mountains,
   From India's coral strand,
Where Afric's sunny fountains
   Roll down their golden sand;
From many an ancient river,
From many a palmy plain,
   They call us to deliver
      Their land from error's chain.

2. Shall we, whose souls are lighted
      With wisdom from on high—
   Shall we, to man benighted,
      The lamp of life deny?
   Salvation, oh, salvation!
      The joyful sound proclaim,
   Till earth's remotest nation
      Has learned Messiah's name.

3. Waft, waft, ye winds, His story,
      And you, ye waters, roll,
   Till, like a sea of glory,
      It spreads from pole to pole;
   Till o'er our ransom'd nature
      The Lamb for sinners slain
   Redeemer, King, Creator,
      In bliss returns to reign. HEBER.

No. 95. Heaven is My Home. 6s & 4s.

1. I'm but a stranger here,
      Heav'n is my home;
   Earth is a desert drear,
      Heav'n is my home;
   Danger and sorrow stand
   Round me on ev'ry hand,
   Heav'n is my fatherland,
      Heav'n is my home.

2. What tho' the tempest rage,
      Heav'n is my home;
   Short is my pilgrimage,
      Heav'n is my home;
   Time's cold and wintry blast
   Soon will be overpast;
   I shall reach home at last,
      Heav'n is my home.

3. There at my Saviour's side,
      Heav'n is my home;
   I shall be glorified,
      Heav'n is my home;
   There are the good and blest,
   Those I loved most and best,
   There, too, I soon shall rest,
      Heav'n is my home.
         THOS. RAWSON TAYLOR.

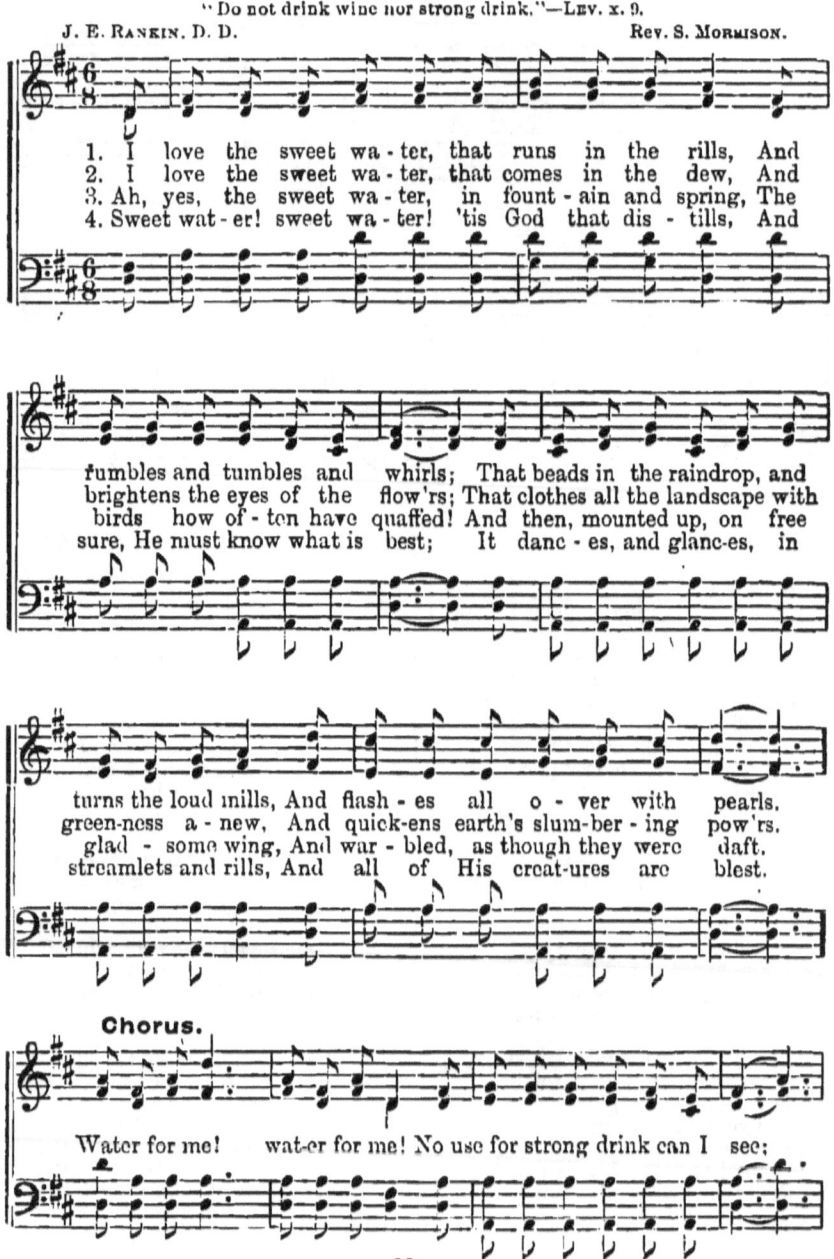

No. 98. The Waters Are Troubled.

"The angel troubled the waters."—JOHN. v. iv.

J. E. RANKIN, D. D. Rev. S. MORRISON.

1. The wa-ters are troubled. The an-gel is here; The fountain of mercy Flows heal-ing and clear; Oh, come in your sorrow, And come in your sin; The wa-ters are troubled: Step in, oh, step in!
2. The wa-ters are troubled, No long-er de-lay; The fountain of mercy, Has heal-ing to-day! Then why will ye ling-er? Since life you may win; The wa-ters are troubled: Step in, oh, step in!
3. The wa-ters are troubled! The first will be healed; The fountain of mercy, A-las! may be sealed: An-oth-er be-fore you, Sal-va-tion may win; The wa-ters are troubled: Step in, oh, step in!
4. The wa-ters are troubled! The an-gel still waits; He paus-es in per-il Who halts and de-bates: Give o-ver your falt'ring, Your struggles with-in; The wa-ters are troubled: Step in, oh, step in!

99. Cross and Crown. C. M.

1. Must Jesus bear the cross alone,
   And all the world go free?
   No; there's a cross for every one,
   And there's a cross for me.

2. How happy are the saints above,
   Who once went sorrowing here;
   But now they taste unmingled love
   And joy without a tear.

3. The consecrated cross I'll bear,
   Till death shall set me free;
   And then go home, my crown to wear,
   For there's a crown for me.

No. 101. I Am the Lord's.

"He is able to keep that which I have committed unto him against that day."—2 Tim. i, 12.

JAMES NICHOLSON. BISHOP W. JOHNS.

1. In Jesus I have found sweet rest, With heav'nly peace my soul is blest;
2. Beneath the shadow of His wings, My soul in ver-y triumph sings;
3. Though clouds of sorrow of-ten come To in-ter-cept my view of home,
4. In life henceforth, thro' grace divine, My lamp well trimm'd shall burn and shine;

My heart with thankfulness o'er flows, Oh, how de-light-ful this re-pose.
Behind His mercies firm and broad, My soul is hid with Christ in God.
By faith a heav'nly light is seen, To gild the gloom that lies between.
In death I'll sing a-bove the flood, That I am saved through Jesus' blood.

Chorus.

I'm bound to Christ by love's sweet cords, Living or dying I am the Lord's;

I'm bound to Christ by love's sweet cords, Oh, yes, I am the Lord's.

No. 103. Loose the Cable, and Let Me Go.

"So he bringeth them to their desired haven."—Ps. cvii. 30.

J. E. RANKIN, D. D.   Rev. S. MORRISON.

1. Fierce the tempest is beating in all the air, The waters are dashing below: While yon haven of rest smiles serene and fair; Loose the cable and let me go.
2. Lord, the night is fast closing around my bark, I long for the break of the day, Near I see there the rocks, all so grim and stark; Speak the word, and I speed away.
3. There's no safety for me on this foreign strand, No peace while so far from my home, I am longing for rest in that fair, fair land; I am waiting till Jesus come.
4. It's far better for me, from this world to part, And be there with Jesus my Lord, Than to linger too long with a weary heart, From His love, and my sure reward.

Chorus.

Let me go, let me go where no tempests beat! Where the

Loose the Cable, and Let Me Go—Concluded.

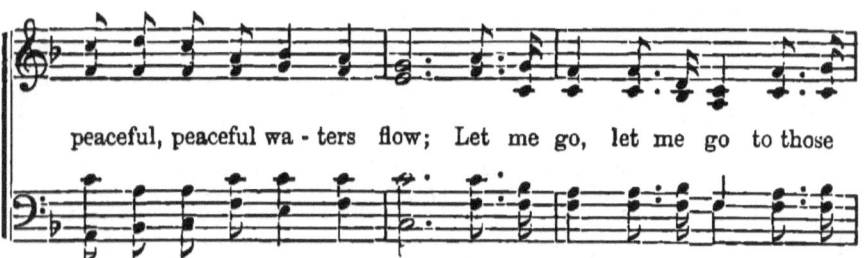

peaceful, peaceful waters flow; Let me go, let me go to those

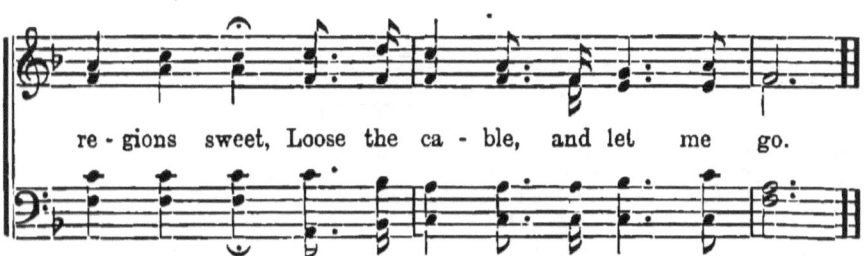

regions sweet, Loose the cable, and let me go.

No. 104. Woodstock. C. M.

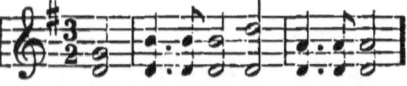

1. I love to steal awhile away
   From every cumbering care,
   And spend the hours of setting day
   In humble, grateful prayer.

2. I love in solitude to shed
   The penitential tear;
   And all His promises to plead
   When none but God is near.

3. I love to think on mercies past,
   And future good implore;
   And all my cares and sorrows cast
   On Him whom I adore.

4. I love by faith to take a view
   Of brighter scenes in heaven;
   The prospect doth my strength renew
   While here by tempests driven.
   BROWN.

No. 105. Coronation. C. M.

1. All hail the power of Jesus' name!
   Let angels prostrate fall;
   Bring forth the royal diadem,
   And crown him Lord of all.

2. Ye chosen seed of Israel's race,
   Ye ransom'd from the fall,
   Hail him who saves you by his grace,
   And crown him Lord of all.

3. Sinners, whose love can ne'er forget
   The wormwood and the gall,
   Go, spread your trophies at his feet,
   And crown him Lord of all.

4. Let every kindred, every tribe,
   On this terrestrial ball,
   To him all majesty ascribe,
   And crown him Lord of all.
   DUNCAN.

No. 106. Obey My Voice, and Drink No Wine.

"We have obeyed the voice of Jonadab, to drink no wine all our days."—JER. 35. 8.

J. E. RANKIN, D. D.   KARL REDEN.

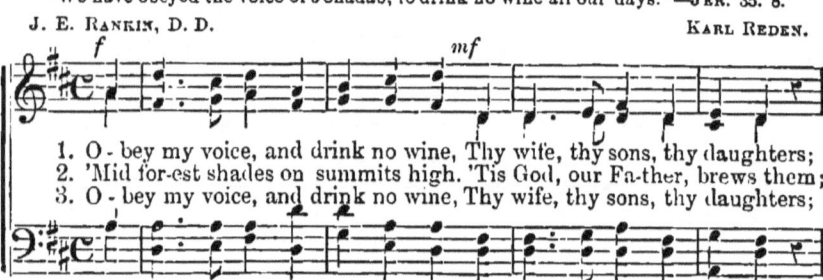

1. O - bey my voice, and drink no wine, Thy wife, thy sons, thy daughters;
2. 'Mid for-est shades on summits high. 'Tis God, our Fa-ther, brews them;
3. O - bey my voice, and drink no wine, Thy wife, thy sons, thy daughters;

But drink, in-stead, the draught di-vine, The sweet, dis-till-ing wa-ters;
The cup he fills, shall we de-ny? The crys-tal streams re-fuse them?
But drink, in-stead, the draught di-vine, The sweet, dis-till-ing wa-ters;

Duet. mf

They pour their tide down mountain's side, And from cool caverns sal-ly;
They bead with health, they bead with wealth, They make the verdant a-cre;
Thou shalt not know the drunkard's woe, His want shall not dis-tress thee;

cres.

They flash so bright in morn-ing's light, They sing a-long the val-ley,
The birds and flow'rs, they bless the show'rs, And know them from their Maker.
But thou shalt stand, prince in the land, And God, thy God, shall bless thee.

Obey My Voice, and Drink No Wine--Concluded.

No. 107. Rest for the Weary.

1. In the Christian's home in glory
   There remains a land of rest;
   There my Saviour's gone before me
   To fulfill my soul's request.
Cho.—There is rest for the weary,
   There is rest for the weary,
   There is rest for the weary,
   There is rest for you;
   On the other side of Jordan,
   In the sweet fields of Eden,
   Where the tree of life is bloom-
   There is rest for you.   [ing,

2. He is fitting up my mansion,
   Which eternally shall stand;
   For my stay shall not be transient
   In that holy, happy land.

3. Pain nor sickness ne'er shall enter,
   Grief nor woe my lot shall share:
   But in that celestial centre
   I a crown of life shall wear.

No. 108. Windham, L, M,

1. Show pity, Lord, O Lord, forgive;
   Let a repenting rebel live;
   Are not thy mercies large and free?
   May not a sinner trust in thee?

2. My crimes are great, but don't surpass
   The power and glory of thy grace;
   Great God, thy nature hath no bound,
   So let thy pard'ning love be found.

3. Oh, wash my soul from every sin,
   And make my guilty conscience clean;
   Here on my heart the burden lies,
   And past offences pain my eyes,

4. My lips with shame my sins confess,
   Against thy law, against thy grace;
   Lord, should thy judgments grow severe,
   I am condemned, but thou art clear.
                                    Watts.

No. 109. Trust, Oh, Trust Your Father.

"Consider the lilies, how they grow."—MATT. vi. 28.

J. E. RANKIN, D. D.   FR. SILCHER:

1. Lo, the li - lies, how they grow, 'Neath Spring rains de-scend-ing;
2. Take no tho't what ye shall eat, Troub - le do not bor-row;
3. Trust, oh, trust your Fa-ther's care, Liv - ing Bread He's giv-en;

'Tis your Fa-ther clothes them so, Their sweet gra-ces blend-ing;
He who gives all crea - tures meat, Will pro - vide to-mor-row;
Rai - ment, too, both white and fair, He pro - vides in heav-en;

Why, then, are ye full of care, Since His love is eve - ry - where?
He who hears the ra - ven's cry, Sure - ly can-not you de - ny;
He will there his work com-plete, For the life is more than meat;

Trust, oh, trust your Fa - ther, Trust, oh, trust your Fa-ther.
Trust, oh, trust your Fa - ther, Trust, oh, trust your Fa-ther.
Trust, oh, trust your Fa - ther, Trust, oh, trust your Fa-ther.

No. 110. Gliding Down Life's River.

"I must work the works of Him that sent me, while it is day."—JOHN ix. 4.

J. E. R. J. E. RANKIN, D. D.

1. In this world of sin and ru-in, Glid-ing down Life's ri-ver, There is work we must be do-ing; Glid-ing down Life's riv-er: Ev-'ry day there's something new, Which the Lord would have us do, Work for me, and work for you. Gliding down Life's river, Gliding down Life's river.

2. We must lift the Cross above us!
   Gliding down Life's river:
   We must work for those who love us,
   Gliding down Life's river;
   We must early toil and late,
   Must obey, and not debate;
   We must pray, and we must wait,
   Gliding down Life's river.

3. We must raise our fallen brother,
   Gliding down Life's river:
   We must help and cheer, each other;
   Gliding down Life's river;
   Where the weak or tempted stand,
   We must heed our Lord's command:
   We must lend a helping hand,
   Gliding down Life's river!

4. We must never faint nor falter,
   Gliding down Life's river:
   What if come, or cross, or halter,
   Gliding down Life's river?
   Let the world make its ado,
   To our Lord we must be true;
   Must be Christian through and through,
   Gliding down Life's river.

5. We must soothe the sick and sighing,
   Gliding down Life's river!
   We must point to Christ the dying,
   Gliding down Life's river;
   We must keep the goal in view:
   Must our Master's steps pursue;
   We must do, what he would do,
   Gliding down Life's river.

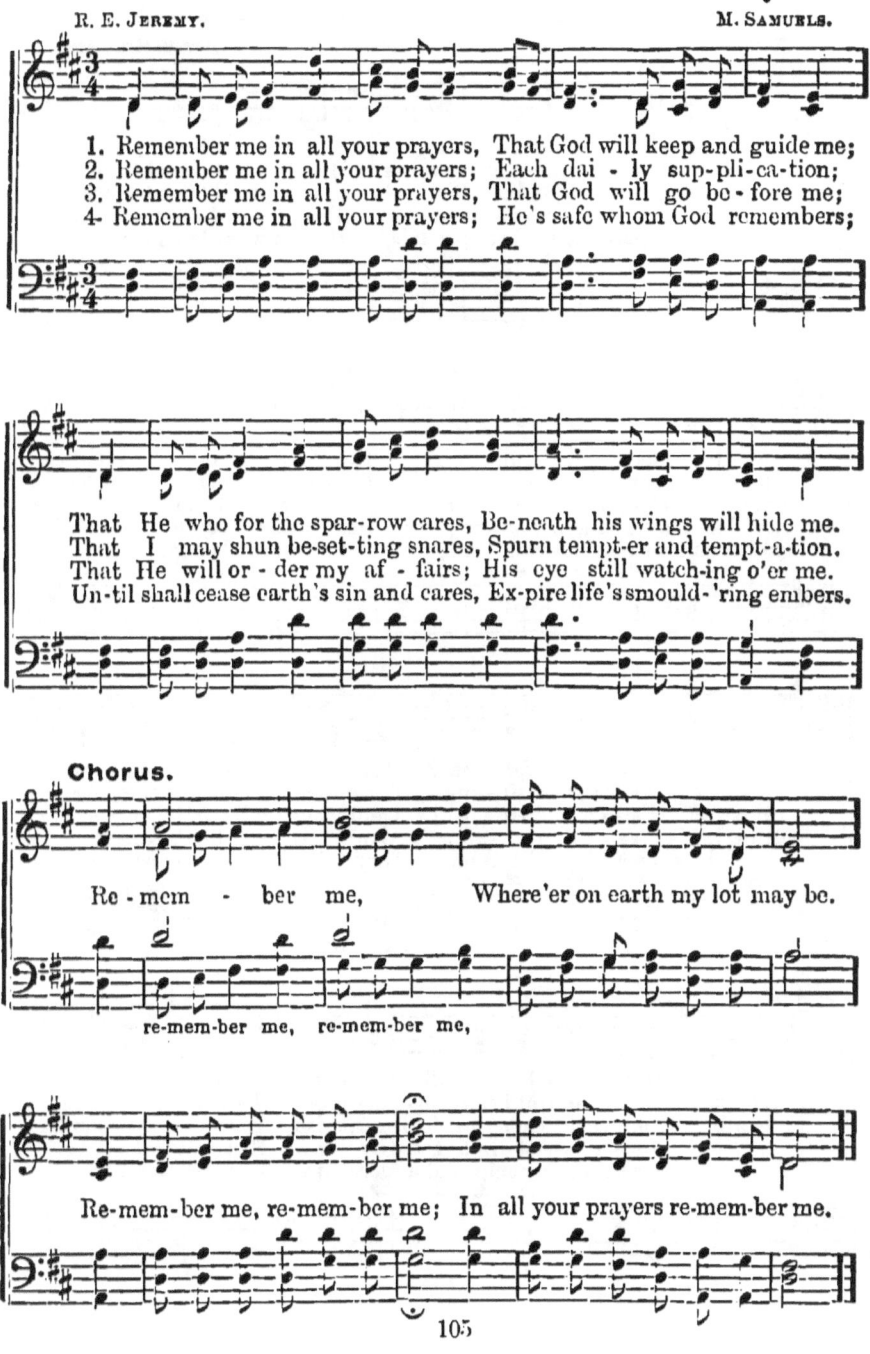

No. 113. Heavenward Bound.

"They desire a better country, that is an heavenly."—HEB. xi. 16.

T. CORBEN, D. D. Rev S. MORRISON.

1. We are pil-grims here and strang-ers, Heav'n-ward bound, What care we for toils and dan - gers; Heav'n-ward bound, What care we for foes in - fer - nal? Christ is ours, the King e-ter - nal, He will lead to fields all ver - nal, Heav'n-ward bound.

2. What care we for cares and cross - es? Heav'n-ward bound, Crook-ed lot or heav - y loss - es; Heav'n-ward bound, There, there's neith - er woe nor wail - ing, There, there's neith-er ache nor ail - ing, In that land of health un - fail - ing, Heav'n-ward bound.

3. We are near the land of Beu - lah, Heav'n-ward bound, Sweet the air; the breeze blows cool - er, Heav'n-ward bound, Land where grapes of Es - chol flour - ish; Land where milk and hon - ey nour-ish; Land where doubts and fears all perish, Heav'n-ward bound.

4. Soon our san-dals hot un - bind - ing, Heav'n-ward bound, Soon our loved and lost, there find - ing, Heav'n-ward bound, We shall drink Life's crys - tal riv - er, We shall eat Life's fruit for - ev - er, We shall see of Life the Giv - er, Heav'n-ward bound.

5. We shall pass the gold-en por-tals, Heav'n-ward bound, Where in white walk love's im - mor - tals, Heav'n-ward bound, Where the rain - bow arch - ing o'er him, They all cast their crowns be - fore Him, Where they wor-ship and a - dore Him, Heav'n-ward bound.

No. 114. Wondrous Whosoever.

"Whosoever will, let him take the waters of life freely."—Rev. xxii. 17.

J. E. Rankin, D. D.
E. S. Lorenz.

1. Who-so-ev-er! O word di-vine! Who-so, who-so-ev-er!
2. Who-so-ev-er! 'Tis Je-sus' word! Word that changeth nev-er:
3. Who-so-ev-er on Christ be-lieves!—With His blood He seals it;
4. Who-so-ev-er! Oh, wondrous thought! Though so high a-bove us;—

Yes, sal-va-tion, it may be thine: May be thine for-ev-er.
Sin-ner lost, hast thou ev-er heard: Who-so, who-so-ev-er?
Free for-give-ness he there re-ceives: 'Tis God's Word re-veals it.
That in spite of sin's crim-son spot, He, the Lord, can love us.

Refrain.

Who-so-ev-er! Oh, wilt thou hear it? Free salvation! and thou art near it!

Who-so-ev-er! Oh, word di-vine! Won-drous who-so-ev-er!

Art Thou Ready?—Concluded.

Art thou read-y?.... Art thou read-y? Do not lin-ger longer, come to-day.

No. 116. A Few More Days.

"Neither shall there be any more pain."—REV. xxi. 4.

J. E. RANKIN, D. D. WALTER N. RANKIN.

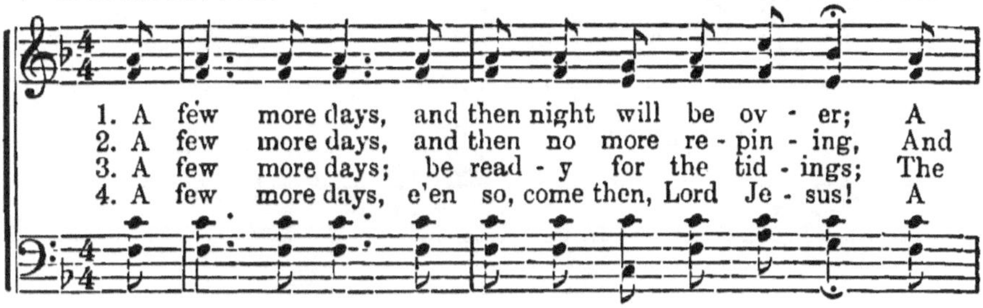

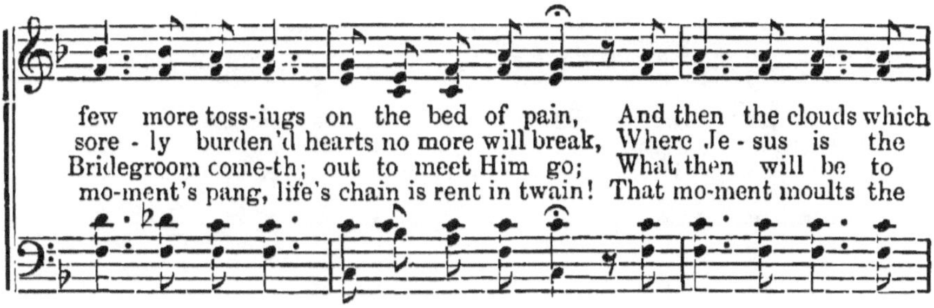

1. A few more days, and then night will be ov - er; A few more toss-ings on the bed of pain, And then the clouds which o'er us dark-ly hov-er, Shall be dis-pelled, not to re-turn a - gain.
2. A few more days, and then no more re - pin - ing, And sore - ly burden'd hearts no more will break, Where Je - sus is the Sun e - ter - nal shin-ing, He'll come, un - to Him-self His own to take.
3. A few more days; be read - y for the tid - ings; The Bridegroom come-th; out to meet Him go; What then will be to thee these human chidings, These bitter cups, that thou shouldst dread them so?
4. A few more days, e'en so, come then, Lord Je - sus! A mo - ment's pang, life's chain is rent in twain! That mo-ment moults the spir-it's wing and frees us For aye from sin and sor-row, and from pain.

Tis Jesus, Only Jesus--Concluded

Chorus.

'Tis Je - sus, on - ly Je - sus, Oh, pur-est, sweet-est bliss!

We then shall look on Je-sus, And see him as he is.

No. 118. Webb. 7s & 6s.

No. 119. Varina. C. M. D.

1. The morning light is breaking,
   The darkness disappears;
   The sons of earth are waking,
   To penitential tears;
   Each breeze that sweeps the ocean
   Brings tidings from afar
   Of nations in commotion,
   Prepared for Zion's war.

2. See heathen nations bending
   Before the God we love,
   And thousand hearts ascending
   In gratitude above;
   While sinners now confessing,
   The Gospel call obey,
   And seek the Saviour's blessing—
   A nation in a day.
   S. F. SMITH.

1. There is a land of pure delight,
   Where saints immortal reign;
   Infinite day excludes the night,
   And pleasures banish pain.
   There everlasting spring abides,
   And never with'ring flowers;
   Death, like a narrow sea divides
   This heavenly land from ours.

2. Sweet fields beyond the swelling flood
   Stand dress'd in living green;
   So to the Jews old Canaan stood.
   While Jordan roll'd between,
   Could we but stand where Moses stood,
   And view the landscape o'er,
   Not Jordan's stream, nor death's cold flood
   Should fright us from the shore.
   WATTS.

No. 122. A Little More Faith in Jesus.

"If thou canst believe; all things are possible to him that believeth."—MARK ix. 22.

T. CORBEN, D. D. REV. S. MORRISON.

1. My burden's great, what can I do? A lit-tle more faith in Je-sus;
2. My pathway's dark, I can-not see, A lit-tle more faith in Je-sus;
3. The struggle's hard, the flesh is weak, A lit-tle more faith in Je-sus;
4. More faith in Him will take us through, A lit-tle more faith in Je-sus;

Ah! that's the trouble with me and with you, A little more faith in Je-sus.
Ah! that's the trouble with you and with me, A little more faith in Je-sus.
Ah! that's the trouble; for strength we must seek A little more faith in Je-sus.
We can do all things; to Him if we're true; A little more faith in Je-sus.

Chorus.

My burden's great, my faith is small, Ah, that's the trouble with us all!

A lit-tle more faith, a lit-tle more faith, A lit-tle more faith in Je-sus.

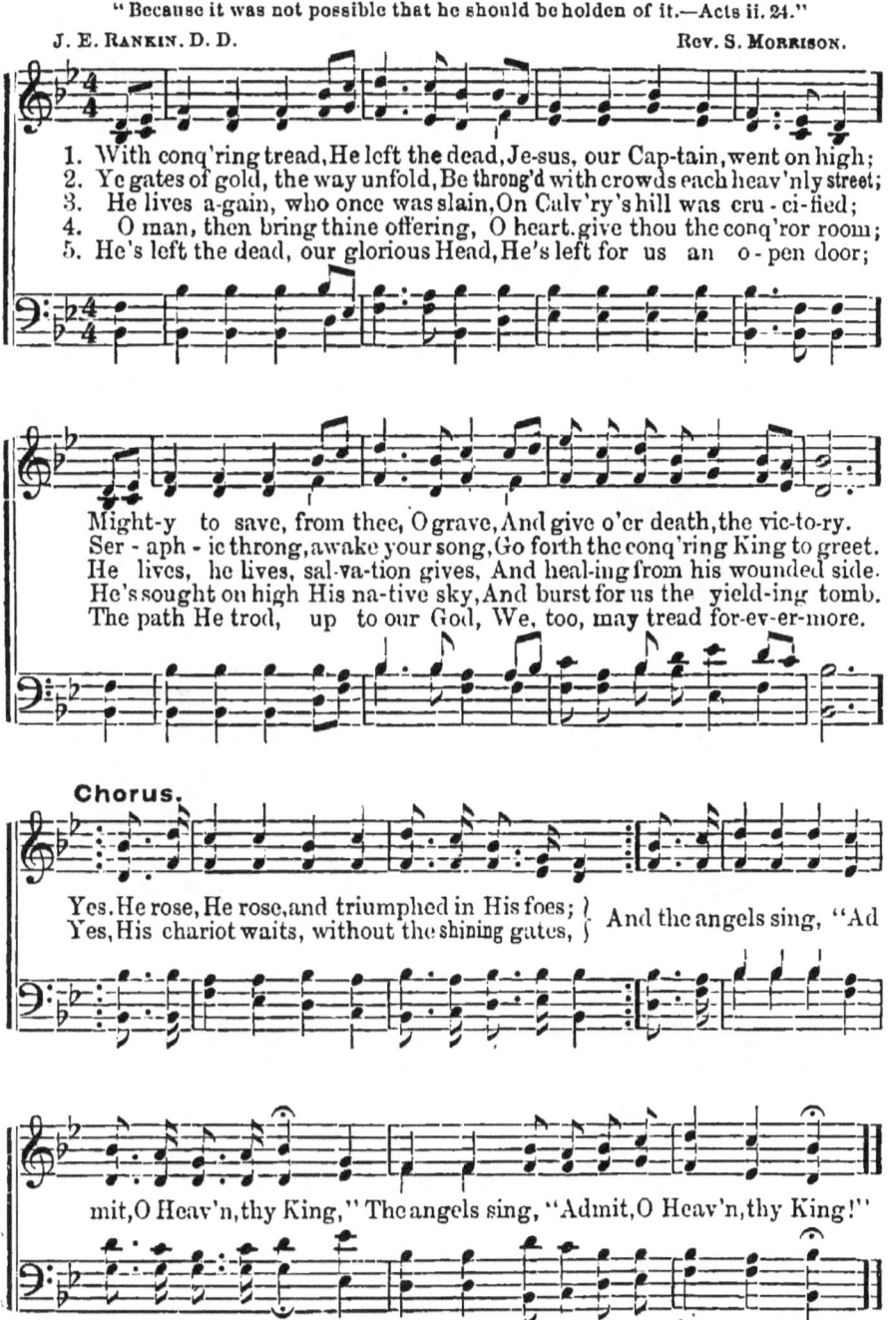

I Will Sing of My King---Concluded.

When He comes all re-splen-dent; With a shout, with a shout,

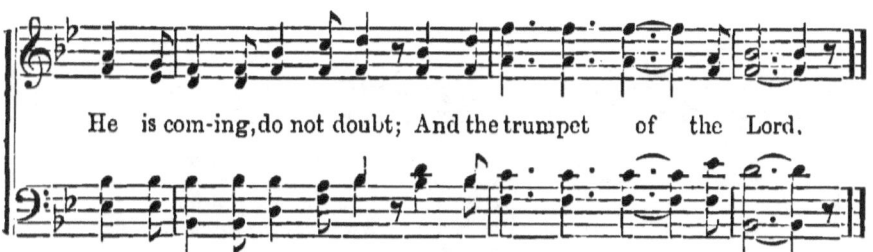

He is com-ing, do not doubt; And the trumpet of the Lord.

No. 125. Hamburg. L. M.

1. Just as I am, without one plea,
 But that thy blood was shed for me,
 And that thou bid'st me come to thee,
 O Lamb of God ! I come, I come.

2. Just as I am, and waiting not
 To rid my soul of one dark blot,
 To thee whose blood can cleanse each spot,
 O Lamb of God ! I come, I come.

3. Just as I am, though tossed about
 With many a conflict, many a doubt,
 Fightings within, and fears without,
 O Lamb of God ! I come, I come.

4. Just as I am, poor, wretched, blind,
 Sight, riches, healing of the mind,
 Yea, all I need, in thee I find,
 O Lamb of God ! I come, I come.

No. 126. The Solid Rock. L. M. 6 lines.

1. My hope is built on nothing less
 Than Jesus' blood and righteousness;
 I dare not trust the sweetest frame,
 But wholly lean on Jesus' name:
 On Christ, the solid rock, I stand;
 All other ground is sinking sand.

2. When darkness seems to veil his face,
 I rest on his unchanging grace;
 In every high and stormy gale,
 My anchor holds within the vail:
 On Christ, the solid rock, I stand;
 All other ground is sinking sand.

3. His oath, his covenant, and blood,
 Support me in the whelming flood;
 When all around my soul gives way,
 He then is all my hope and stay:
 On Christ, the solid rock, I stand;
 All other ground is sinking sand.
 REV. EDWARD MOTE.

No. 129. Sweet, Sweet the Bells Ring.

"If thou call the Sabbath a delight, the holy of the Lord honorable."—Is. lviii. 13.

J. E. RANKIN, D. D.
Rev. S. MORRISON.

1. Though we're glad to laugh and play, Still we love the Lord's own day;
2. There we read God's ho-ly Word, There we learn to know the Lord,
3. Pure, and true, and un-de-filed, Be on earth each Christian child,
4. May these lit-tle er-ring feet, Walk at last the gold-en street,

Sweet, sweet the bells ring, Round, round the bells swing, As we
Sweet, sweet the bells ring, Round, round the bells swing, As we
Sweet, sweet the bells ring, Round, round the bells swing, As we
Sweet, sweet the bells ring, Round, round the bells swing, As we

rise and we hast-en a - way; Balm is on the morning air;
rise and we hast-en a - way; There we sit and sing God's praise,
rise and we hast-en a - way; Pure as when the lil-y blows,
rise and we hast-en a - way; May we all be-fore God stand,

'Tis the day of praise and pray'r, Sweet, sweet the bells ring, Round, round the bells swing
Guide our feet in Wisdom's ways, Sweet, sweet, etc.
Sweet as Sha-ron's fra-grant rose, Sweet, sweet, etc.
In that sweet, sweet Canaan Land, Sweet, sweet, etc.

Sweet, Sweet the Bells Ring—Concluded.

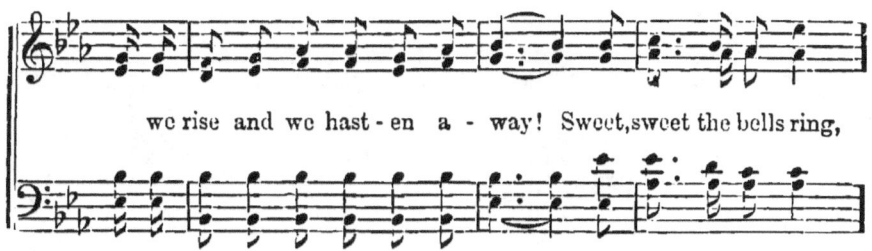

we rise and we hast-en a-way! Sweet, sweet the bells ring,

Round, round the bells swing, As we rise and we hast-en a-way-

130. Lenox. H. M.

1. Blow ye the trumpet, blow
   The gladly solemn sound;
   Let all the nations know,
   To earth's remotest bound,
   The year of Jubilee is come;
   Return, ye ransomed sinners, home.

2. Jesus, our great High Priest,
   Has full atonement made;
   Ye weary spirits rest;
   Ye mourning souls be glad;
   The year of Jubilee is come;
   Return, ye ransomed sinners, home.

3. Exalt the Lamb of God,
   The sin-atoning Lamb;
   Redemption by his blood
   Through all the world proclaim;
   The year of Jubilee is come;
   Return, ye ransomed sinners, home.
   TOPLADY.

131. Kentucky. S. M.

1. A charge to keep I have,
   A God to glorify;
   A never-dying soul to save
   And fit it for the sky.

2. To serve the present age,
   My calling to fulfill—
   O may it all my powers engage,
   To do my Master's will.

3. Arm me with jealous care,
   As in thy sight to live:
   And O, thy servant, Lord, prepare,
   A strict account to give.

4. Help me to watch and pray,
   And on thyself rely,
   Assured, if I my trust betray,
   I shall forever die.
   Rev. C. WESLEY.

No. 133. Toplady. 7s, 6 lines.

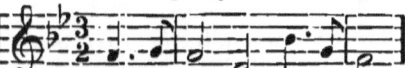

1. Rock of ages, cleft for me,
   Let me hide myself in thee;
   Let the water and the blood
   From thy wounded side which flow'd,
   Be of sin the double cure—
   Save from wrath and make me pure.

2. Could my tears forever flow,
   Could my zeal no languor know,
   These for sin could not atone;
   Thou must save, and thou alone;
   In my hand no price I bring;
   Simply to thy cross I cling.

3. While I draw this fleeting breath,
   When my eyes shall close in death,
   When I rise to worlds unknown,
   And behold thee on thy throne,
   Rock of ages, cleft for me,
   Let me hide myself in thee.

No. 134. Missionary Chant. L. M.

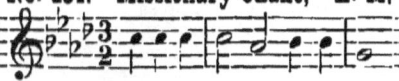

1. Ye Christian heralds, go proclaim
   Salvation in Immanuel's name;
   To distant climes the tidings bear,
   And plant the rose of Sharon there.

2. He'll shield you with a wall of fire,
   With holy zeal your hearts inspire,
   Bid raging winds their fury cease,
   And calm the savage breast to peace.

3. And when our labors all are o'er,
   Then shall we meet to part no more—
   Meet with the blood-bought throng to fall,
   And crown the Saviour Lord of all.

No. 135. America. 6s & 4s.

1. God bless our native land!
   Firm may she ever stand,
      Through storm and night;
   When the wild tempests rave,
   Ruler of winds and wave,
   Do thou our country save
      By thy great might.

2. For her our prayer shall rise
   To God, above the skies;
      On him we wait:
   Thou who art ever nigh,
   Guarding with watchful eye,
   To thee aloud we cry,
      God save the State!

No. 136. Over There.

1. Oh, think of the home over there,
   By the side of the river of light,
   Where the saints all immortal and fair,
   Are robed in their garments of white.
   REF.—Over there, over there,
      Oh, think of the home over there.

3. Oh, think of the friends over there,
   Who before us the journey have trod,
   Of the song that they breathe on the air,
   In their home in the palace of God.

3. My Saviour is now over there,
   There my kindred and friends are at rest;
   Then away from my sorrow and care,
   Let me fly to the land of the blest,

4. I'll soon be at home over there,
   For the end of my journey I see;
   Many dear to my heart, over there,
   Are watching and waiting for me.

No. 137. Sweet Hour of Prayer.

1. Sweet hour of prayer! sweet hour of prayer!
   That calls me from a world of care,
   And bids me at my Father's throne,
   Make all my wants and wishes known
   In seasons of distress and grief,
   My soul has often found relief,
   And oft escaped the tempter's snare,
   By thy return, sweet hour of prayer;
   And oft escaped the tempter's snare,
   By thy return, sweet hour of prayer;

2. Sweet hour of prayer! sweet hour of prayer!
   May I thy consolation share,
   Till from Mount Pisgah's lofty height
   I view my home, and take my flight;
   This robe of flesh I'll drop, and rise
   To seize the everlasting prize;
   And shout, while passing through the air,
   Farewell, farewell, sweet hour of prayer.

No. 138. Shepherd. 8s, 7s & 4s.

1. Saviour, like a shepherd lead us,
   Much we need thy tenderest care;
   In thy pleasant pastures feed us,
   For our use thy folds prepare.
   Blessed Jesus, blessed Jesus,
   Thou hast bought us, thine we are;
   Blessed Jesus, blessed Jesus,
   Thou hast bought us, thine we are.

2. We are thine, do thou befriend us,
   Be the Guardian of our way;
   Keep thy flock, from sin defend us,
   Seek us when we go astray.
   Blessed Jesus, blessed Jesus,
   Hear young children when they pray.

No. 139. Nettleton.

1. Come, thou fount of every blessing,
   Tune my heart to sing thy grace;
   Streams of mercy, never ceasing,
   Call for songs of loudest praise.
   Teach me some melodious sonnet,
   Sung by flaming tongues above;
   Praise the mount—I'm fixed upon it;
   Mount of thy redeeming love!

2. O! to grace how great the debtor,
   Daily I'm constrained to be!
   Let thy goodness, like a fetter,
   Bind my wand'ring heart to thee.
   Prone to wander, Lord, I feel it—
   Prone to leave the God I love;
   Here's my heart, O take and seal it!
   Seal it for thy courts above.

No. 140. Cleansing Wave.

1. Oh, now I see the cleansing wave,
   The fountain deep and wide;
   Jesus, my Lord, mighty to save,
   Points to his wounded side,
   CHORUS.
   The cleansing stream, I see, I see!
   I plunge, and, oh, it cleanseth me!
   Oh, praise the Lord! it cleanseth me!
   It cleanseth me—yes, cleanseth me.

2. I see the new creation rise,
   I hear the speaking blood;
   It speaks! polluted nature dies!
   Sinks 'neath the cleansing flood.

No. 141. Joy to the World.

1. Joy to the world, the Lord is come!
   Let earth receive her King;
   Let every heart prepare him room,
   And heaven and nature sing.

2. No more let sin and sorrow grow,
   Nor thorns infest the ground;
   He comes to make his blessings flow
   Far as the curse is found.

No. 142. The Race for Glory.

1. Awake my soul! stretch every nerve,
   And press with vigor on;
   A heavenly race demands thy zeal,
   And an immortal crown.

2. 'Tis God's all-animating voice
   That calls thee from on high;
   'Tis he whose hand presents the prize
   To thine aspiring eye.

No. 143. The Convert. 12s & 9s.

1. O how happy are they
   Who the Saviour obey,
   And have laid up their treasures above;
   Tongue can never express
   The sweet comfort and peace
   Of a soul in its earliest love.

2. That sweet comfort was mine,
   When the favor divine
   I received through the blood of the Lamb;
   When my heart first believed,
   What a joy I received—
   What a heaven in Jesus' name

3. 'Twas a heaven below
   My Redeemer to know,
   And the angels could do nothing more
   Than to fall at his feet,
   And the story repeat,
   And the Lover of sinners adore

No 144. Trusting.

1. I am coming to the cross;
   I am poor, and weak, and blind;
   I am counting all but dross,
   I shall full salvation find.
   CHORUS.
   I am trusting, Lord in thee,
   Dear Lamb of Calvary;
   Humbly at thy cross I bow,
   Save me, Jesus, save me now.

2. Here I give my all to thee,
   Friends, and time, and earthly store;
   Soul and body, thine to be,—
   Wholly thine forevermore

No. 145. Stockwell. 8s & 7s.
1. Silently the shades of evening
Gather round our chapel door;
Silently they bring before us
Faces we shall see no more.
2. Sweet the moments, rich in blessing,
Which before the cross I spend;
Life, and health and peace possessing,
From the sinner's dying friend.
3. Oh, the lost, the unforgotten!
Though the world be oft forgot!
Oh, the shrouded and the lonely!
In our hearts they perish not.

No. 146. Retreat. L. M.
1. From every stormy wind that blows,
From every swelling tide of woes,
There is a calm, a sure retreat—
'Tis found beneath the mercy-seat.
2. There is a place where Jesus sheds
The oil of gladness on our heads,
A place, than all besides more sweet,
It is the blood-bought mercy-seat.
. There, there on eagles' wings we soar,
And sin and sense molest no more;
And Heaven comes down our souls to greet,
While glory crowns the mercy-seat.

No. 147. Siloam. C. M.
1. By cool Siloam's shady rill,
How sweet the lily grows!
How sweet the breath, beneath the
Of Sharon's dewy rose! [hill,
2. Lo! such the child whose early feet
The paths of peace have trod—
Whose secret heart, with influence
Is upward drawn to God. [sweet,
3. Oh, thou who givest life and breath,
We seek thy grace alone,
In childhood, manhood, age, and death,
To keep us still thine own.

No. 148. All Paid.
1. I hear the Saviour say,
Thy strength indeed is small;
Child of weakness, watch and pray,
Find in me thine all in all.
CHORUS.
Jesus paid it all,
All to him I owe;
Sin hath left a crimson stain;
He washed it white as snow.
2. For nothing good have I
Whereby thy grace to claim—
I'll wash my garment white
In the blood of Calvary's Lamb.
3. When from my dying bed
My ransomed soul shall rise,
Then "Jesus paid it all"
Shall rend the vaulted skies.
4. And when before the throne
I stand in him complete,
I'll lay my trophies down,
All down at Jesus' feet.

No. 149. I Love to Tell the Story.
1. I love to tell the story
Of unseen things above,
Of Jesus and his glory,
Of Jesus and his love.
I love to tell the story,
Because I know it's true;
It satisfies my longings
As nothing else would do.
CHORUS.
I love to tell the story,
'Twill be my theme in glory
To tell the old, old story
Of Jesus and his love.
2. I love to tell the story:
More wonderful it seems
Than all the golden fancies
Of all our golden dreams.
I love to tell the story,
It did so much for me,
And that is just the reason
I tell it now to thee.

No. 150. Olivet.
1. My faith looks up to thee,
Thou Lamb of Calvary:
Saviour divine!
Now hear me while I pray,
Take all my guilt away,
Oh, let me from this day
Be wholly thine.
2. May thy rich grace impart
Strength to my fainting heart,
My zeal inspire:
As thou hast died for me
Oh, may my love to thee
Pure, warm, and changeless be—
A living fire.
3. While life's dark maze I tread,
And griefs around me spread,
Be thou my guide;
Bid darkness turn to day;
Wipe sorrow's tears away,
Nor let me ever stray
From thee aside.

INDEX.

TITLES IN SMALL CAPS—FIRST LINES IN ROMAN.

A

A charge to keep I have........... 131
A FEW MORE DAYS............... 116
A LITTLE MORE FAITH IN JESUS... 122
All hail the power of Jesus' name.. 105
All paid.....................No. 148
ALL PRAISE AND ALL MAJESTY.... 20
Anything Thou sendeth me........ 52
AMERICA.......................... 135
ANYWHERE WE'LL WORK FOR HIM. 117
ART THOU READY?................ 115
ART THOU LONGING?.............. 13
ARIEL............................. 68
ARE YOU READY, CHILDREN, READY? 14
Around the throne of God........ 8
AS I AM, O JESUS, TAKE ME....... 28
Awake, my soul, stretch every nerve. 142

B

BE THOU FAITHFUL................ 44
BEAUTIFUL THE LITTLE HANDS.... 15
BEHOLD HOW SWEET.............. 54
Believe in Jesus wherever you are.. 70
BETHANY......................... 36
BEYOND THE RIVER............... 81
Blest be the tie that binds......... 39
BLESSED JESUS................... 56
Blow ye the trumpet, blow........ 130
Brother, hast thou wandered far?. 92
By cool Siloam's shady rill....... 147

C

CAN YOU POINT A LOST ONE TO THE
  SAVIOUR?...................... 9
CHRIST IS PRECIOUS.............. 120
CLEANSING WAVE................. 140
Come listen dear children........ 47
COME NEAR ME, O MY SAVIOUR... 89
COME SIGN THE PLEDGE TO-NIGHT. 26
Come, thou fount of every blessing. 139
COME, TREMBLING SOUL.......... 63
COME, YE DISCONSOLATE......... 40
CORONATION..................... 105
CROSS AND CROWN................ 99
Crown the Saviour with your praises 2
CROWN HIM, YE CHILDREN; JESUS
  IS KING....................... 2

D

DENNIS........................... 39
DRIFTING AWAY................... 76

E

ETERNITY......................... 57

F

FAITH............................ 29
Fair freedom's land.............. 49
FALLING FEATHERS................ 82
FATHER, BLESS OUR SCHOOL TO-DAY 87
Fierce the tempest is beating...... 103
FLING IT OUT, THE ROYAL BANNER. 3
FOUNTAIN......................... 78
FREDERIC......................... 69
FRIEND THE SWEETEST............ 31
Friends we have beyond the river.. 81
From every stormy wind that blows. 146
From Greenland's icy mountain... 94

G

GLIDING DOWN LIFE'S RIVER...... 110
GLORY BE TO JESUS' NAME........ 73
Glory, glory be to Jesus.......... 73
GO WASH IN THE STREAM......... 25
GOD BE WITH YOU................ 50
God bless our native land........ 135
GOOD-BYE TILL WE MEET IN THAT
  FAR OFF LAND................. 132

H

HAMBURG......................... 125
HE CARETH FOR YOU.............. 70
Hear the ringing bells of gladness. 30
HEBRON........................... 56
Heaven is to me no foreign strand.. 37
HEAVEN IS MY HOME.............. 95
HEAVENWARD BOUND.............. 113
HIDING IN THEE.................. 83
How CAN I BUT LOVE HIM?....... 35
How goes the battle, brother?..... 44

I

I am sitting at thy board......... 7
I AM PRAYING FOR YOU........... 17
I have a Saviour................. 17
I AM THE LORD'S................. 101

	Number.
I'm but a stranger here	95
I'M REDEEMED; BOUGHT WITH A PRICE	51
I'LL SING FOR JESUS	24
I'll sing of that stream	25
I am coming to the cross	144
I CANNOT SING AS ANGELS SING	12
I do not ask for the pride of earth	18
I have read of a beautiful city	45
I LOVE THE DEAR SAVIOUR	34
I LONG TO BE THERE	67
I have found repose for my weary soul	91
I hear the Saviour say	148
I love the sweet water	96
I love to steal awhile away	104
I LOVE TO TELL THE STORY	149
I sing of a city	4
I think, when I read that sweet story	79
I WILL SING OF MY KING	124
I was a wandering sheep	72
I would not live alway	69
I've a home far away	67
In some way or other the Lord will provide	5
In the path I'm walking	16
In the darkest hour	33
In Jesus I have found sweet rest	101
In the Christian's home in glory	107
In this world of sin and ruin	110
IS IT THERE, WRITTEN THERE	18
IT IS I, O SOUL DISMAYED	13

J

JESUS ALL THE WAY	77
Jesus, and shall it ever be	56
Jesus, friend of all, the sweetest	31
Jesus, lover of my soul	60
JESUS IS CALLING THEE	21
Jesus shed his precious blood	51
Just as I am	125
JOY TO THE WORLD	141

K

KENTUCKY	131

L

LEBANON	72
LENOX	130
Like faithful soldiers	88
LITTLE SOLDIERS	88
LITTLE CHILDREN, CAN YOU TELL	100
Lo, the lilies, how they grow	109
Lo, THE HARVEST IS WHITE	102

M

Mamma, said little Nellie	82
MARTYN	60
MAY A LITTLE TENDER LAMB	111
MISSIONARY CHANT	134

	NUMBER.
MISSIONARY HYMN	94
Must Jesus bear the Cross alone	99
My burden's great, what can I do	122
My days are gliding swiftly by	38
My hope is built on nothing less	126
MY HEAVENLY HOME	4
My faith looks up to Thee	150

N

Nearer my God to Thee	36
NEARER TO THEE	42
NETTLETON	139
Not for its walls of Jasper	117
NOT HALF HAS EVER BEEN TOLD	45

O

O how happy I should be	55
O PRODIGAL, DON'T STAY AWAY	80
O how happy are they	143
Obey my voice and drink no wine	106
Oh, could I speak the matchless worth	68
OH, HAD I WINGS LIKE A DOVE	48
Oh, hearken, dear Saviour	86
Oh, land of all earth's land, the best	49
Oh, safe to the rock	83
OUR HIDING PLACE	23
OVER THERE	136
Oh, think of a home over there	136
Oh, now I see the cleansing wave	140
OLIVET	150

P

PLEYEL'S HYMN	92
PRECIOUS IS THE NAME OF JESUS	53

R

Reapers! O reapers	102
REFUGE	33
REMEMBER ME IN ALL YOUR PRAYERS	112
REPEAT THE SWEET STORY	27
REST FOR THE WEARY	107
RETREAT	146
Rock of Ages cleft for me	133

S

Saviour, like a shepherd, lead us	138
SEE YE NOT THE HOSTILE LEGIONS	90
Shall I sing a song of my king	124
SHALL WE GATHER AT THE RIVER	65
SHINING SHORE	38
Show pity, Lord, O Lord, forgive	108
Silently the shades of evening	145
SILOAM	146
SIR, WE WOULD SEE JESUS	6
So tender, so precious	85
Soon the ev'ning shadows falling	115
STOCKWELL	145
SWEET CANAAN LAND	37
SWEET HOUR OF PRAYER	137

	NUMBER.
Sweet, Sweet the Bells Ring	129

T

	NUMBER.
Tell Me More, Still More, of Jesus	1
That Beautiful Land	93
The Bells of Gladness	80
The Door of God's Mercy is Open	85
The First Christmas Below	47
The Golden Gate of Prayer	43
The King Who is Greatest	59
The Gospel Bells	64
The King's Highway	75
The Lord Will Provide	5
The Lord is My Light	62
The Path of the Just	16
The prize is set before us	46
The Race for Glory	142
There's a Better Time A-Coming	58
There's a far away beautiful land	93
There is a fountain filled with blood	78
There is a happy land	66
There's a land far away	132
There's a land of pure delight	119
There Is One True and Only God	84
There is a refuge now I know	23
The sky is overcast	29
The Sweet Story	79
The Solid Rock	126
The Waters Are Troubled	98
The Wee Lambs of the Fold	80
The White-Robed Angels	22
The Wide, Wide World	19
They tell me there are dangers	19
Thou Knowest All Things; Is it I	7
Thou art walking, O my Saviour	11
Though we're glad to laugh and play	129
'Tis Jesus when the burdened heart	77

	NUMBER.
'Tis Jesus, Only Jesus	117
To-day the Saviour calls	41
Toplady	133
Triumph By-and-By	46
Trusting	144
Trusting in the Promise	91
Trust, Oh, Trust Your Father	109

U

Unto the Lamb	8

V

Varina	119

W

Water for Me	96
We are pilgrims here, and strangers	113
We Shall Meet Them	10
What a friend we have in Jesus	71
What Shall I Do for the Master	126
When I Walk Thro' the Valley	74
When Jesus, our Saviour	6
When We Lose Our Dear Ones	
White as Snow	32
Wherever you may be	75
Here	97
Whosoever, O word divine	114
Why wilt thou not relent	57
Why should the heathen oppose Him	59
Will the white-robed angels meet us	22
With Conquering Tread He Left the Dead	123
Work, for the night is coming	61
Woodstock	104
Wondrous Whosoever	114
Wyndham	108

Y

Ye Christian heralds	134

www.ingramcontent.com/pod-product-compliance
Lightning Source LLC
Chambersburg PA
CBHW021939160426
43195CB00011B/1144